AMERICAN SKETCHES

LECTOR HOUSE PUBLIC DOMAIN WORKS

AMERICAN SKETCHES

CHARLES WHIBLEY

ISBN: 978-93-90387-37-3

Published: 1908

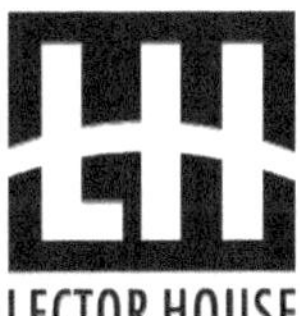

LECTOR HOUSE LLP
E-MAIL: lectorpublishing@gmail.com

AMERICAN SKETCHES

BY

CHARLES WHIBLEY

1908

CONTENTS

AMERICAN SKETCHES.

NEW YORK.

To land at Hoboken in a quiet drizzle is to sound the depths of desolation. A raw, half-finished, unkempt street confronts you. Along the roadway, roughly broken into ruts, crawls a sad tram. The dishevelled shops bear odd foreign-looking names upon their fronts, and the dark men who lounge at their doors suggest neither the spirit of hustling nor the grandeur of democracy. It is, in truth, not a street, but the awkward sketch of a street, in which all the colours are blurred and the lines drawn awry. And the sense of desolation is heightened by the memory of the immediate past. You have not yet forgotten the pomp of a great steamship. The gracious harbour of New York is still shining in your mind's eye. If the sentiment of freedom be dear to you, you are fresh from apostrophising the statue of Liberty, and you may have just whispered to yourself that you are breathing a clearer, larger air. Even the exquisite courtesy of the officer who has invited you in the blandest terms to declare that you have no contraband, has belied the voice of rumour and imparted a glow of satisfaction. And then you are thrown miserably into the leaden despair of Hoboken, and the vision of Liberty herself is effaced.

But Hoboken is an easy place where-from to escape, and the traveller may pass through it the more cheerfully, because it prepares him for the manifold and bewildering contrasts of New York. The towns of the old world have alternations of penury and affluence. In them also picturesque squalor obtrudes itself upon an ugly splendour. But New York, above all other cities, is the city of contrasts. As America is less a country than a collection of countries, so New York is not a city—it is a collection of cities. Here, on the narrow rock which sustains the real metropolis of the United States, is room or men and women of every faith and every race. The advertisements which glitter in the windows or are plastered upon the hoardings suggest that all nationalities meet with an equal and a flattering acceptance. The German regrets his fatherland the less when he finds a brilliant Bier-Halle waiting for his delight. The Scot no doubt finds the "domestic" cigar sweeter to his taste if a portrait of Robert Burns adorns the box from which he takes it. The Jew may be supposed to lose the sense of homesickness when he can read the news of every day in his familiar Yiddish. And it is not only in the contrast of nationalities that New York proves its variety. Though Germans, Italians, and Irish inhabit their own separate quarters and frequent their own separate haunts, there are many other lines of division. Nowhere in the world are there sharper, crueller distinctions of riches and poverty, of intelligence and boorish-ness, of beauty and ugliness. How, indeed, shall you find a formula for a city which contains within its larger boundaries Fifth Avenue and the Bowery, the Riverside Drive and Brooklyn, Central Park and Coney Island?

And this contrast of race and character is matched by the diversity of the city's aspect. Its architecture is as various as its inhabitants. In spite of demolition and utility, the history of New York is written brokenly upon its walls. Here and there you may detect an ancient frame-house which has escaped the shocks of time and chance, and still holds its own against its sturdier neighbours. Nor is the memory of England wholly obliterated. Is there not a homely sound in Maiden Lane, a modest thoroughfare not far from Wall Street? What Englishman can feel wholly abroad if he walk out to the Battery, or gaze upon the austere houses of Washington Square? And do not the two churches of Broadway recall the city of London, where the masterpieces of Wren are still hedged about by overshadowing office and frowning warehouse? St Paul's Chapel, indeed, is English both in style and origin. It might have been built in accord with Sir Christopher's own design; and, flanked by the thirty-two storeys of the Park Row Building, it has the look of a small and dainty toy. Though Trinity Church, dedicated to the glory of God and the Astors, stands in an equally strange environment, it is less incongruous, as it is less elegant, than St Paul's. Its spire falls not more than a hundred feet below the surrounding sky-scrapers, and were it not for its graveyard it might escape notice. Now its graveyard is one of the wonders of America. Rich in memories of colonial days, it is as lucid a piece of history as survives within the boundaries of New York. The busy mob of cosmopolitans, intent upon trusts and monopolies, which passes its time-worn stones day after day, may find no meaning in its tranquillity. The wayfarer who is careless of the hours will obey the ancient counsel and stay a while. The inscriptions carry him back to the days before the Revolution, or even into the seventeenth century. Here lies one Richard Churcher, who died in 1681, at the tender age of five. And there is buried William Bradford, who printed the first newspaper that ever New York saw, the forefather in a long line of the Yellowest Press on earth. And there is inscribed the name of John Watts, the last Royal Recorder of New York. Thus the wayfarer may step from Broadway into the graveyard of a British colony, and forget, in contemplating the familiar examples of a lapidary style, that there was a tea-party at Boston.

These contrasts are wayward and accidental. The hand of chance has been merciful, that is all; and if you would fully understand New York's self-conscious love of incongruity it is elsewhere that you must look. Walk along the Riverside Drive, framed by nature to be, what an enthusiast has called it, "the finest residential avenue in the world." Turn your back to the houses, and contemplate the noble beauty of the Hudson River. Look from the terrace of Claremont upon the sunlit scene, and ask yourself whether Paris herself offers a gayer prospect. And then face the "high-class residences," and humble your heart. Nowhere else will you get a clearer vision of the inappropriateness which is the most devoutly worshipped of New York's idols. The human mind cannot imagine anything less like "residences" than these vast blocks of vulgarity. The styles of all ages and all countries have been recklessly imitated. The homes of the millionaires are disguised as churches, as mosques, as medieval castles. Here you may find a stronghold of feudalism cheek by jowl with the quiet mansion of a colonial gentleman. There Touraine jostles Constantinople; and the climax is reached by Mr Schwab, who has decreed for himself a lofty pleasure-dome, which is said to resemble Chambord, and which takes its place in a long line of villas, without so much as a turnip-field to give it an air of seclusion or security. In this vainglorious craving for discomfort there is a kind of naïveté which is not without its pathos. One proud lady, whose husband, in the words of a dithyrambic guide-book, "made a fortune from a patent glove-hook," boasts that her mansion has a glass-room on the second floor. Another vain householder deems it sufficient to proclaim that he spent two million dollars upon the villa which shelters him from the storm. In brief, there is scarcely a single palace on the Riverside which may not be described as an antic of wealth, and one wonders what sort of a life is lived within these gloomy walls. Do the inhabitants dress their parts with conscientious gravity, and sit down to dine with the trappings of costume and furniture which belong to their houses? Suppose they did, and, suppose in obedience to a signal they precipitated themselves upon the highway, there would be such a masquerade of fancy dress as the world has never seen. The Riverside Drive, then, is a sermon in stones, whose text is the uselessness of uncultured dollars. If we judged New York by this orgie of tasteless extravagance, we might condemn it for a parvenu among cities, careless of millions and sparing of discretion. We may not thus judge it New York, if it be a parvenu, is often a parvenu of taste, and has given many a proof of intelligence and refinement. The home of great luxury, it does not always, as on the Riverside, mistake display for beauty. There are houses in the neighbourhood of Fifth Avenue which are perfect in reticence and suitability. The clubs of New York are a splendid example even to London, the first home of clubs. In Central Park the people of New York possesses a place of amenity and recreation which Europe cannot surpass; and when you are tired of watching the antics of the leisurely chipmunk, who gambols without haste and without fear, you may delight in a collection of pictures which wealth and good management will make the despair and admiration of the world. Much, of course, remains to do, and therein New York is fortunate. Her growing interest in sculpture and architecture is matched by a magnificent opportunity. In the Old World all has been accomplished. Our buildings are set up, our memorials dedicated, our pictures gathered into galleries. America starts, so to say, from scratch; there is no limit to her ambition; and she has infinite money. If the past is ours, the future is hers, and we may look forward to it with curiosity and with hope.

The architects of America have not only composed works in accordance with the old traditions and in obedience to ancient models; they have devised a new style and a new method of their own. To pack a vast metropolis within a narrow space, they have made mountains of houses. When the rock upon which their city stands proved insufficient for their ambition, they conquered another kingdom in the air. The skyscrapers which lift their lofty turrets to the heaven are the pride of New York. It is upon them that the returning traveller gazes most eagerly, as he nears the shore. They hold a firmer place in his heart than even the Statue of Liberty, and the vague sentiment which it inspires. With a proper vanity he points out to the poor Briton, who shudders at five storeys, the size and grandeur of his imposing palaces. And his arrogance is just. The sky-scraper presents a new view of architecture. It is original, characteristic, and beautiful. Suggested and enforced, as I have said, by the narrowness of the rock, it is suitable to its atmosphere and environment. New York is a southern, sunlit city, which needs protection from the heat and need not fear obscurity. Even where the buildings are highest, the wayfarer does not feel that he is walking at the bottom of a well. But, let it be said at once, the sky-scraper would be intolerable in our grey and murky land. London demands a broad thoroughfare and low houses. These are its only defence against a covered sky and an enveloping fog, and the patriotic Americans who would transplant their sky-scrapers to England merely prove that they do not appreciate the logic and beauty of their own design.

What, then, is a sky-scraper? It is a giant bird-cage, whose interstices are filled with stone or concrete. Though its structure is concealed from the eye, it is impossible not to wonder at its superb effrontery. It depends for its effect, not upon ornament, which perforce appears trivial and inapposite, but upon its mass. Whatever approaches it of another scale and kind is dwarfed to insignificance. The Sub-Treasury of the United States, for instance, looks like a foolish plaything beside its august neighbours. Where sky-scrapers are there must be no commemorative statues, no monuments raised to merely human heroes. The effigy of Washington in Wall Street has no more dignity than a tin soldier. And as the skyscraper makes houses of a common size ridiculous, so it loses its splendour when it stands alone. Nothing can surpass in ugliness the twenty storeys of thin horror that is called the Flat-iron; and it is ugly because it is isolated in Madison Square, a place of reasonable dimensions. It is continuity which imparts a dignity to these mammoths. The vast masses which frown upon Wall Street and Broadway are austere, like the Pyramids. They seem the works of giants, not of men. They might be a vast phenomenon of nature, which was before the flood, and which has survived the shocks of earthquake and the passage of the years. And when their summits are lit by the declining sun, when their white walls look like marble in the glow of the reddening sky, they present such a spectacle as many a strenuous American crosses the ocean to see in Switzerland, and crosses it in vain.

New York, in truth, is a city of many beauties, and with a reckless prodigality she has done her best to obscure them all. Driven by a vain love of swift traffic, she assails your ear with an incessant din and your eye with the unsightliest railroad that human ingenuity has ever contrived. She has sacrificed the amenity of her streets and the dignity of her buildings to the false god of Speed. Why men worship Speed, a demon who lies in wait to destroy them, it is impossible to understand. It would be as wise and as profitable to worship Sloth. However, the men of New York, as they tell you with an insistent and ingenuous pride, are "hustlers." They must ever be moving, and moving fast. The "hustling," probably, leads to little enough. Haste and industry are not synonymous. To run up and down is but a form of busy idleness. The captains of industry who do the work of the world sit still, surrounded by bells and telephones. Such heroes as J. Pierpont Morgan and John D. Rockefeller are never surprised on train or trolley. They show themselves furtively behind vast expanses of plate-glass, and move only to eat or sleep. It is the common citizen of New York who is never quiet. He finds it irksome to stay long in the same place. Though his house may be comfortable, even luxurious, he is in a fever to leave it. And so it comes about that what he is wont to call "transportation" seems the most important thing in his life. We give the word another signification. To New York it means the many methods of conveying passengers from one point to another. And the methods, various as they are, keep pace with the desires of the restless citizen, who may travel at what pace and altitude he desires. He may burrow, like a rabbit, beneath the ground. If he be more happily normal in his tastes he may ride in a surface car. Or he may fly, like a bird through the air, on an overhead railway. The constant rattle of cars and railways is indescribable. The overhead lines pass close to the first-floor windows, bringing darkness and noise wherever they are laid. There are offices in which a stranger can neither hear nor be heard, and yet you are told that to the accustomed ear of the native all is silent and reposeful. And I can easily believe that a sudden cessation of din would bring an instant madness. Nor must another and an indirect result of the trains and trams which encircle New York be forgotten. The roads are so seldom used that they are permitted to fall into a ruinous decay. Their surface is broken into ruts and yawns in chasms. To drive "down-town" in a carriage is to suffer a sensation akin to sea-sickness; and having once suffered, you can understand that it is something else than the democratic love of travelling in common that persuades the people of New York to clamber on the overhead railway, or to take its chance in a tram-car.

Movement, then, noisy and incessant, is the passion of New York. Perhaps it is the brisk air which drives men to this useless activity. Perhaps it is no better than an ingrained and superstitious habit. But the drowsiest foreigner is soon caught up in the whirl. He needs neither rest nor sleep. He, too, must be chasing something which always eludes him. He, too, finds himself leaving a quiet corner where he would like to stay, that he may reach some place which he has no desire to see. Even though he mount to the tenth or the twentieth story, the throb of the restless city reaches him. Wall Street is "hustling" made concrete. The Bowery is crowded with a cosmopolitan horde which is never still. Brooklyn Bridge and Brooklyn Ferry might be the cross-roads of the world. There a vast mob is passing hither and thither, on foot, on boats, on railroads. What are they doing, whither are they going, these scurrying men and women? Have they no business to pursue, no office-stool to sit upon, no typewriting machines to jostle? And when you are weary of transportation, go into the hall of a big hotel and you will find the same ceaseless motion. On all sides you will hear the click, click of telephone and telegram. On all sides you will see eager citizens scanning the tape, which brings them messages of ruin or success. Nowhere, save in a secluded bar or a stately club, will you find a single man content to be alive and to squander the leisure that God has given him.

And with all her undying haste New York is not content. She must still find other means of saving time. And to save time she has strained all the resources of civilisation. In that rather dismal thing called "material progress" she is easily

ahead of the world. Never was the apparatus of life so skilfully turned and handled as in New York. There are no two fixed points which are not easily connected
by iron lines. There seems no reason why a citizen of New York should ever walk.
If stairs exist, he need not use them, for an express lift, warranted not to stop before
the fifteenth floor, will carry him in a few seconds to the top of the highest building.
If he open a cupboard door, the mere opening of it lights an electric lamp, and he
need not grope after a coat by the dim light of a guttering candle. At his bed-head
stands a telephone, and, if he will, he may speak to a friend a thousand miles away
without moving from his pillow. But time is saved—of that there is no doubt. The
only doubt is, whether it be worth saving. When New York has saved her time,
what does she do with it? She merely squanders it in riotous movement and reckless "transportation." Thus she lives in a vicious circle—saving time that she may
spend it, and spending it that again she may save it. Nor can this material progress
be achieved without a loss of what the Old World prizes most highly. To win all
the benefits which civilisation affords, you must lose peace and you must sacrifice
privacy. The many appliances which save our useless time may be enjoyed only by
crowds. The citizens of New York travel, live, and talk in public. They have made
their choice, and are proud of it Englishmen are still reckless enough to waste their
time in pursuit of individualism, and I think they are wise. For my part, I would
rather lose my time than save it, and the one open conveyance of New York which
in pace and conduct suits my inclination is the Fifth Avenue Stage.

But New York is unique. It baffles the understanding and defies observation.
In vain you search for a standard of comparison. France and England set out many
centuries ago from the same point and with the same intention. America has nothing in common, either of purpose or method, with either of these countries. To a
European it is the most foreign city on earth. Untidy but flamboyant, it is reckless
of the laws by which life is lived elsewhere. It builds beautiful houses, it delights in
white marble palaces, and it thinks it superfluous to level its roads. Eager for success, worshipping astuteness as devoutly as it worships speed, it is yet indifferent
to the failure of others, and seems to hold human life in light esteem. In brief, it is a
braggart city of medieval courage and medieval cruelty, combining the fierceness
of an Italian republic with a perfect faith in mechanical contrivance and an ardent
love of material progress.

Here, then, are all the elements of interest and curiosity. Happy are the citizens who watch from day to day the fight that never before has been fought on the
same terms. And yet more strangely baffling than the city are the citizens. Who are
they, and of what blood and character? What, indeed, is a New Yorker? Is he Jew
or Irish? Is he English or German? Is he Russian or Polish? He may be something
of all these, and yet he is wholly none of them. Something has been added to him
which he had not before. He is endowed with a briskness and an invention often
alien to his blood. He is quicker in his movement, less trammelled in his judgment
Though he may lose wisdom in sharpening his wit, the change he undergoes is
unmistakable. New York, indeed, resembles a magic cauldron. Those who are cast
into it are born again. For a generation some vague trace of accent or habit may
remain. The old characteristics must needs hang about the newly-arrived immi-

grant. But in a generation these characteristics are softened or disappear, and there is produced a type which seems remote from all its origins. As yet the process of amalgamation is incomplete, and it is impossible to say in what this hubble-shubble of mixed races will result. Nor have we any clue of historical experience which we may follow. The Roman Empire included within its borders many lands and unnumbered nationalities, but the dominant race kept its blood pure. In New York and the other great cities of America the soil is the sole common factor. Though all the citizens of the great republic live upon that soil, they differ in blood and origin as much as the East of Europe differs from the West. And it is a mystery yet un-pierced that, as the generations pass, they approach nearer and nearer to uniformity, both in type and character. And by what traits do we recognise the citizen of New York? Of course there is no question here of the cultivated gentleman, who is familiar in Paris and London, and whose hospitality in his own land is an amiable reproach to our own too frequent thoughtlessness, but of the simpler class which confronts the traveller in street and train, in hotel and restaurant. The railway guard, the waiter, the cab-driver—these are the men upon whose care the comfort of the stranger depends in every land, and whose tact and temper are no bad index of the national character. In New York, then, you are met everywhere by a sort of urbane familiarity. The man who does you a service, for which you pay him, is neither civil nor uncivil. He contrives, in a way which is by no means unpleasant, to put himself on an equality with you. With a mild surprise you find yourself taking for granted what in your own land you would resent bitterly. Not even the curiosity of the nigger, who brushes your coat with a whisk, appears irksome. For the habit of years has enabled white man and black to assume a light and easy manner, which in an Englishman, born and trained to another tradition, would appear impertinence.

And familiarity is not the only trait which separates the plain man of New York from the plain man of London. The New Yorker looks upon the foreigner with the eye of patronage. To his superior intelligence the wandering stranger is a kind of natural, who should not be allowed to roam alone and at large. Before you have been long in the land you find yourself shepherded, and driven with an affability, not unmixed with contempt, into the right path. Again, you do not resent it, and yet are surprised at your own forbearance. A little thought, however, explains the assumed superiority. The citizen of New York has an ingenuous pride and pleasure in his own city and in his own prowess, which nothing can daunt. He is convinced, especially if he has never travelled beyond his own borders, that he engrosses the virtue and intelligence of the world The driver of a motor-car assured me, with a quiet certitude which brooked no contradiction, that England was cut up into sporting estates for the "lords," and that there the working man was doomed to an idle servility. "But," said he, "there is no room for bums here." This absolute disbelief in other countries, combined with a perfect confidence in their own, has persuaded the citizens of New York to look down with a cold and pitiful eye upon those who are so unfortunate as to be born under an effete monarchy. There is no bluster in their attitude, no insistence. The conviction of superiority is far too great for that. They belong to the greatest country upon earth; they alone enjoy the true blessings of freedom; they alone understand the dignity of labour and the spirit of in-dependence; and they have made up their minds kindly but firmly that you shall not forget it.

Thus you carry away from New York a memory of a lively air, gigantic buildings, incessant movement, sporadic elegance, and ingenuous patronage. And when you have separated your impressions, the most vivid and constant impression that remains is of a city where the means of life conquer life itself, whose citizens die hourly of the rage to live.

BOSTON.

America, the country of contrasts, can show none more sudden or striking than that between New York and Boston. In New York progress and convenience reach their zenith. A short journey carries you back into the England of the eighteenth century. The traveller, lately puzzled by overhead railways and awed by the immensity of sky-scrapers, no sooner reaches Boston than he finds himself once more in a familiar environment. The wayward simplicity of the city has little in common with the New World. Its streets are not mere hollow tubes, through which financiers may be hastily precipitated to their quest for gold. They wind and twist like the streets in the country towns of England and France. To the old architects of Boston, indeed, a street was something more than a thoroughfare. The houses which flanked it took their places by whim or hazard, and were not compelled to follow a hard immovable line. And so they possess all the beauty which is born of accident and surprise. You turn a corner, and know not what will confront you; you dive down a side street, and are uncertain into what century you will be thrust. Here is the old wooden house, which recalls the first settlers; there the fair red-brick of a later period. And everywhere is the diversity which comes of growth, and which proves that time is a better contriver of effects than the most skilful architect.

The constant mark of Boston is a demure gaiety. An air of quiet festivity encompasses the streets. The houses are elegant, but sternly ordered. If they belong to the colonial style, they are exquisitely symmetrical. There is no pilaster without its fellow; no window that is not nicely balanced by another of self-same shape and size. The architects, who learned their craft from the designs of Inigo Jones and Christopher Wren, had no ambition to express their own fancy. They were loyally obedient to the tradition of the masters, and the houses which they planned, plain in their neatness, are neither pretentious nor inappropriate. Nowhere in Boston will you find the extravagant ingenuity which makes New York ridiculous; nowhere will you be disturbed by an absurd mimicry of exotic styles; nowhere are you asked to wonder at mountainous blocks of stone. Boston is not a city of giants, but of men who love their comfort, and who, in spite of Puritan ancestry, do not disdain to live in beautiful surroundings. In other words, the millionaire has not laid his iron hand upon New England, and, until he come, Boston may still boast of its elegance.

The pride of Boston is Beacon Street, surely one among the most majestic streets in the world. It recalls Piccadilly and the frontage of the Green Park. Its broad spaces and the shade of its dividing trees are of the natural beauty which time alone can confer, and its houses are worthy its setting. I lunched at the Somerset Club, in a white-panelled room, and it needed clams and soft-shell crabs to convince me that I was in a new land, and not in an English country-house. All was of another time and of a familiar place—the service, the furniture, the aspect. And was it possible to regard our sympathetic hosts as strange in blood or speech?

The Mall, in Beacon Street, if it is the pride, is also the distinguishing mark of Boston. For Boston is a city of parks and trees. The famous Common, as those might remember who believe that America sprang into being in a night, has been sacred for nearly three hundred years. Since 1640 it has been the centre of Boston. It has witnessed the tragedies and comedies of an eventful history. "There," wrote an English traveller as early as 1675, "the gallants walk with their marmalet-madams, as we do in Moorfields."

There malefactors were hanged; there the witches suffered in the time of their persecution; and it is impossible to forget, as you walk its ample spaces, the many old associations which it brings with it from the past.

For it is to the past that Boston belongs. No city is more keenly conscious of its origin. The flood of foreign immigration has not engulfed it. Its memories, like its names, are still of England, New and Old. The spirit of America, eagerly looking forward, cruelly acquisitive, does not seem to fulfil it The sentiment of its beginning has outlasted even the sentiment of a poignant agitation. It resembles an old man thinking of what was, and turning over with careful hand the relics of days gone by. If in one aspect Boston is a centre of commerce and enterprise, in another it is a patient worshipper of tradition, It regards the few old buildings which have survived the shocks of time with a respect which an Englishman can easily understand, but which may appear extravagant to the modern American. The Old South Meeting-House, to give a single instance, is an object of simple-hearted veneration to the people of Boston, and the veneration is easily intelligible. For there is scarcely an episode in Boston's history that is not connected, in the popular imagination, with the Old South Meeting-House. It stands on the site of John Winthrop's garden; it is rich in memories of Cotton and Increase Mather. Within its ancient walls was Benjamin Franklin christened, and the building which stands to-day comes down to us from 1730, and was designed in obedient imitation of English masters. There, too, were enacted many scenes in the drama of revolution; there it was that the famous tea-party was proposed; and thence it was that the Mohawks, drunk with the rhetoric of liberty, found their way to the harbour, that they might see how tea mixed with salt-water. If the sentiment be sometimes exaggerated, the purpose is admirable, and it is a pleasant reflection that, in a country of quick changes and historical indifference, at least one building will be preserved for the admiration of coming generations.

It is for such reasons as these that an Englishman feels at home in Boston. He is secure in the same past; he shares the same memories, even though he give them a different interpretation. Between the New and Old England there are more points of similarity than of difference. In each are the same green meadows, the same ample streams, the same wide vistas. The names of the towns and villages in the new country were borrowed from the old some centuries ago; everywhere friendly associations are evoked; everywhere are signs of a familiar and kindly origin. When Winthrop, the earliest of the settlers, wrote to his wife, "We are here in a paradise," he spoke with an enthusiasm which is easily intelligible. And as the little colony grew, it lived its life in accord with the habit and sentiment of the mother-country. In architecture and costume it followed the example set in Bristol or in London. Between these ports and Boston was a frequent interchange of news and commodities. An American in England was no stranger. He was visiting, with sympathy and understanding, the home of his fathers. The most distinguished Bostonians of the late eighteenth century live upon the canvases of Copley, who, in his son, gave to England a distinguished Chancellor, and whose career is the best proof of the good relations which bound England to her colony. Now Copley arrived in England in 1774, when his native Boston was aroused to the height of her sentimental fury, and he was received with acclamation. He painted the portraits of Lord North and his wife, who, one imagines, were not regarded in Boston with especial favour. The King and Queen gave him sittings, and neither political animosity nor professional rivalry stood in the way of his advancement. His temper and character were well adapted to his career. Before he left New England he had shown himself a Court painter in a democratic city. He loved the trappings of life, and he loved to put his sitters in a splendid environment. His own magnificence had already astonished the grave Boston-ians; he is described, while still a youth, as "dressed in a fine maroon cloth, with gilt buttons"; and he set the seal of his own taste upon the portraiture of his friends.

I have said that Boston loves relics. The relics which it loves best are the relics of England's discomfiture. The stately portraits of Copley are of small account compared to the memorials of what was nothing else than a civil war. Faneuil Hall, the Covent Garden of Boston, presented to the city by Peter Faneuil some thirty years before the birth of "Liberty," is now but an emblem of revolt. The Old South Meeting-Place is endeared to the citizens of Boston as "the sanctuary of freedom." A vast monument, erected a mere quarter of a century ago, commemorates the "Boston Massacre." And wherever you turn you are reminded of an episode which might easily be forgotten. To an Englishman these historical landmarks are inoffensive. The dispute which they recall aroused far less emotion on our side the ocean than on the other, and long ago we saw the events of the Revolution in a fair perspective. In truth, this insistence on the past is not wholly creditable to Boston's sense of humour. The passionate paeans which Otis and his friends sang to Liberty were irrelevant. Liberty was never for a moment in danger, if Liberty, indeed, be a thing of fact and not of watchwords. The leaders of the Revolution wrote and spoke as though it was their duty to throw off the yoke of the foreigner,—a yoke as heavy as that which Catholic Spain cast upon Protestant Holland.

But there was no yoke to be thrown off, because no yoke was ever imposed, and Boston might have celebrated greater events in her history than that which an American statesman has wisely called "the glittering and sounding generalities of natural right."

However, if you would forget the follies of politicians, you have but to cross the bridge and drive to Cambridge, which, like the other Cambridge of England, is the seat of a distinguished university. You are doubly rewarded, for not merely is

Cambridge a perfect specimen of a colonial village, but in Harvard there breathes the true spirit of humane letters. Nor is the college a creation of yesterday. It is not far short of three centuries ago that John Harvard, once of Emmanuel College in England, endowed the university which bears his honoured name. The bequest was a poor £780, with 260 books, but it was sufficient to ensure an amiable immortality, and to bestow a just cause of pride upon the mother-college. The daughter is worthy her august parentage. She has preserved the sentiment of her birth; she still worships the classics with a constant heart; the fame of her scholars has travelled in the mouths of men from end to end of Europe. And Harvard has preserved all the outward tokens of a university. Her wide spaces and lofty avenues are the fit abode of learning. Her college chapel and her college halls could serve no other purpose than that for which they are designed. The West, I believe, has built universities on another plan and to another purpose. But Harvard, like her great neighbour Boston, has been obedient to the voice of tradition, and her college, the oldest, remains also the greatest in America.

Culture has always been at once the boast and the reproach of Boston. A serious ancestry and the neighbourhood of a university are enough to ensure a grave devotion to the things of the spirit, and Boston has never found the quest of gold sufficient for its needs. The Pilgrim Fathers, who first sought a refuge in New England, left their country in the cause of what they thought intellectual freedom, and their descendants have ever stood in need of the excitement which nothing save pietism or culture can impart. For many years pietism held sway in Boston. The persecution of the witches, conducted with a lofty eloquence by Cotton Mather, was but the expression of an imperious demand, and the conflict of warring sects, which for many years disturbed the peace of the city, satisfied a craving not yet allayed. Then, after a long interval, came Transcendentalism, a pleasant mixture of literature and moral guidance, and to-day Boston is as earnest as ever in pursuit of vague ideals and soothing doctrines.

But pietism has gradually yielded to the claim of culture. Though one of the largest buildings which frown upon the wayfarer in Boston is a temple raised to the honour of Christian Science and Mrs Eddy, literature is clearly the most fashionable anodyne. It is at once easier and less poignant than theology: while it imparts the same sense of superiority, it suggests the same emancipation from mere world-liness. It is by lectures that Boston attempts to slake its intellectual thirst—lectures on everything and nothing. Science, literature, theology—all is put to the purpose. The enterprise of the Lowell Institute is seconded by a thousand private ventures. The patient citizens are always ready to discuss Shakespeare, except when Tennyson is the subject of the last discourse, and zoology remains attractive until it be obscured by the newest sensation in chemistry. And the appetite of Boston is unglutted and insatiable. Its folly is frankly recognised by the wise among its own citizens. Here, for instance, is the testimony of one whose sympathy with real learning is evident. "The lecture system," says he, "in its best estate an admirable educational instrument, has been subject to dreadful abuse. The unbounded appetite of the New England communities for this form of intellectual nourishment has tempted vast hordes of charlatans and pretenders to try their fortune in this profitable field. 'The hungry sheep look up, and are not fed.' The pay of the lecturer has grown more exorbitant in proportion to the dilution of his mixture, until professional jokers have usurped the places once graced by philosophers and poets; and to-day the lyceums are served by a new species of broker, who ekes out the failing literary material with the better entertainment of music and play-acting."

I am not sure whether the new species of broker is not better than the old. So long as music and play-acting do not masquerade in the worn-out duds of intellect, they do not inflict a serious injury upon the people. It is culture, false and unashamed, that is the danger. For culture is the vice of the intelligence. It stands to literature in the same relation as hypocrisy stands to religion. A glib familiarity with names does duty for knowledge. Men and women think it no shame to play the parrot to lecturers, and to pretend an acquaintance with books whose leaves they have never parted. They affect intellect, when at its best it is curiosity which drives them to lecture hall or institute — at its worst, a love of mental dram-drinking. To see manifest in a frock-coat a poet or man of science whose name is printed in the newspapers fills them with a fearful enthusiasm. To hear the commonplaces of literary criticism delivered in a lofty tone of paradox persuades them to believe that they also are among the erudite, and makes the sacrifice of time and money as light as a wind-blown leaf. But their indiscretion is not so trivial as it seems. Though every man and every woman has the right to waste his time (or hers) as may seem good, something else besides time is lost in the lecture hall. Sincerity also is squandered in the grey, dim light of sham learning, and nobody can indulge in a mixed orgie of "culture" without some sacrifice of honesty and truth.

Culture, of course, is not the monopoly of Boston. It has stretched its long arm from end to end of the American continent. Wherever you go you will hear, in tram or car, the facile gossip of literature. The whole world seems familiar with great names, though the meaning of the names escapes the vast majority. Now the earnest ones of the earth congregate in vast tea-gardens of the intellect, such as Chautauqua. Now the summer hotel is thought a fit place in which to pick up a smattering of literature or science; and there is an uneasy feeling abroad that what is commonly known as pleasure must not be unalloyed. The vice, unhappily, is not unknown in England. A country which had the ingenuity to call a penny reading "university extension," and to send its missionaries into every town, cannot be held guiltless. But our poor attempts at culture dwindle to a paltry insignificance in the light of American enterprise; and we would no more compare the achievement of England in the diffusion of learning with the achievement of the United States, than we would set a modest London office by the side of the loftiest sky-scraper in New York. America lives to do good or evil on a large scale, and we lag as far behind her in culture as in money-making.

When I left Boston for the West, I met in the train an earnest citizen of a not uncommon type. He was immensely and ingenuously patriotic. Though he had never left his native land, and had therefore an insufficient standard of comparison, he was convinced that America was superior in arms and arts to every other part of the habitable globe. He assured me, with an engaging simplicity, that Americans were braver, more energetic, and richer than Englishmen; that, as their buildings were higher, so also were their intelligence and their aspirations. He pointed out that in the vast continent of the West nothing was lacking which the mind of man could desire. Where, he asked, would you find harvests so generous, mines so abundant in precious metals, factories managed with so splendid an ingenuity? If wine and oil are your quest, said he, you have but to tap the surface of the munificent earth. One thing only, he confessed, was lacking, and that need a few years would make good. "Wait," said he, with an assured if immodest boastful-ness,— "wait until we get a bit degenerate, and then we will produce a Shakespeare"! I had not the heart to suggest that the sixteenth century in England was a period of birth, not of decay. I could only accept his statement in awful appreciation. And emboldened by my silence, he supported his argument with a hundred ingeniously chosen facts. He was sure that America would never show the smallest sign of decadence until she was tired of making money. The love of money was the best defence against degeneracy of every kind, and he gasped with simple-hearted pride when he thought of the millions of dollars which his healthy, primitive compatriots were amassing. But, he allowed, the weariness of satiety might overtake them; there might come a time when the ledger and counting-house ceased to be all-sufficient, and that moment of decay would witness the triumph of American literature. "Ben Jonson, Goldsmith, and those fellows," he asked, "lived in a degenerate age, didn't they?" I assented hastily. How could I contradict so agreeable a companion, especially as he was going, as fast as the train could carry him, to take a rest cure?

Such is one victim of the passion for culture. He had probably read nothing in his life save the newspapers and Dickens's 'American Notes,' a work to which he referred with the bitterest resentment. But he had attended lectures, and heard names, some of which remained tinkling in his empty head. To his confused mind English literature was a period of degeneracy, one and indissoluble, in which certain famous writers lived, devoting what time they could snatch from the practice of what he called the decadent vices to the worship of the bottle. There was no harm in him. He was, as the common phrase has it, his own enemy. But he would be better employed in looking at a game of baseball than in playing with humane letters, and one cannot but regret that he should suffer thus profoundly from a vicious system. Another victim of culture comes to my mind. He, too, was from Boston, and as his intelligence was far deeper than the other one's, his unhappiness was the greater. I talked to him for a long day, and he had no conversation but of books. For him the visible world did not exist. The printed page was the beginning and the end of existence. He had read, if not wisely, at least voraciously, and he displayed a wide and profound acquaintance with modern biography. He had all the latest *Lives* at his finger-tips. He knew where all our great contemporaries lived, and who were their friends; he had attended lectures on every conceivable subject; withal he was of a high seriousness, which nothing could daunt. For him, as is but natural, the works of Mr Arthur Benson held the last "message" of modern literature. He could not look upon books as mere instruments of pleasure or enjoyment. He wanted to extract from them that mysterious quality called "help" by the elect of the lecture hall; and without the smallest persuasion he told me which authors had "helped" him in his journey through the world. Shelley, of course, stood first on the list, then came Walt Whitman, and Pater was not far from the top. And there was nothing more strange in this apostle of aesthetics than his matter-of-fact air. His words were the words of a yearning spirit. His tone was the tone of a statistician. Had he really read the books of which he spoke? Did they really "help" him in the making of money, which was the purpose of his life, or did they minister to a mind diseased? I do not know. But I do know that there was a kind of pathos in his cold anxiety. Plainly he was a man of quick perception and alert intelligence. And he seemed to have wasted a vast amount of time in acquiring a jargon which certainly was not his own, and in attaching to books a meaning and purpose which they have never possessed.

Such are two widely different products of the lecture hall, and it is impossible not to see that, widely as their temperaments differ, they have been pushed through the same mill. And thus we arrive at the worst vice of enforced culture. Culture is, like the overhead railroad, a mere saviour of time. It is the tramway of knowledge which compels all men to travel by the same car, whatever may be their ultimate destination. It possesses all the inconvenience of pleasures taken or duties performed in common. The knowledge which is sincere and valuable must be acquired by each man separately; it must correspond to the character and disposition of him who acquires it, or it is a thin disguise of vanity and idleness. To what, then, may we attribute this passion for the lecture hall? Perhaps it is partly due to the provincialism characteristic of America, and partly to an invincible energy, which quickens the popular ambition and urges men to acquire information as they acquire wealth, by the shortest route, and with the smallest exertion.

Above all, culture is the craving of an experimental age, and America no doubt will outgrow it domination. Even now Boston, its earliest slave, is shaking off the yoke; and it is taking refuge in the more modern cities of the West. Chicago is, I believe, its newest and vastest empire. There, where all is odd, it is well to be thought a "thinker." There, we are told, the elect believe it their duty "to reach and stimulate others." But wherever culture is found Strange things are done in its name, and the time may come when by the light of Chicago's brighter lamp Boston may seem to dwell in the outer darkness.

CHICAGO.

America may be defined as the country where there are no railway porters. You begin a journey without ceremony; you end it without a welcome. No zealot, eager to find you a corner seat and to dispose of your luggage, meets you when you depart. You must carry your own bag when you stumble unattended from the train. This enforced dependence upon yourself is doubtless a result of democracy. The spirit of freedom, which permits a stealthy nigger to brush your hat, does not allow another to handle your luggage. To the enchained and servile mind of an Englishman these distinctions axe difficult to understand. A training in transatlantic liberty is necessary for their appreciation. However, no great evil is inflicted on the traveller. The ritual of checking your baggage may easily be learned, and the absence of porters has, by a natural process, evolved the "grip." The "grip," in fact, is the universal mark of America. It is as intimate a part of the citizen's equipment as a hat or coat, and it is not without its advantages. It is light to carry, it fills but a small space, and it ensures that the traveller shall not be separated from all his luggage. A far greater hardship than the carriage of a "grip" is the enforced publicity of an American train. The Englishman loves to travel in seclusion. The end of his ambition is a locked compartment to himself. Mr Pullman has ordained that his clients shall endure the dust and heat of a long journey in public; and when the voyager, wearied out by the rattle of the train, seeks his uncomfortable couch, he is forced to seek it under the general gaze.

These differences of custom are interesting, because they correspond to differences of temperament. There is a far deeper difference in the character of the country through which you travel. A journey in Europe is like a page of history. You pass from one century to another. You see a busy world through the window. As you sit in your corner a living panorama is unfolded before your eyes. The country changes with the sky. Town and mountain and cornfield follow one another in quick succession. At every turn you see that wonderful symbol of romance, the white road that winds over the hill, flecked perhaps by a solitary traveller. But it is always the work of man, not the beauty of nature, that engrosses you. You would, if you could, alight at every point to witness the last act of comedy, which is just beginning. Men and women, to whom you are an episode or an obstruction, flash by. Here is a group of boys bathing. There peasants gaze at the train as something inhuman. At the level crossing a horse chafes in his shafts. In an instant you are whizzed out of sight, and he remains. Then, as night falls, the country-side leaves its work; the eyes of the cottages gleam and flicker through the trees. Round the corner you catch sight of a village festival. The merry-go-rounds glint and clank under the shadow of a church. The mountains approach and recede; streams grow into mighty rivers. The grey sky is dark blue and inlaid with stars. And you sit still, tired and travel-stained, having shared in a day the life of hundreds.

Such is a journey in Europe. How different the experience in America! On the road to Chicago you pass through a wilderness. The towns are infrequent; there are neither roads nor hedges; and the rapidly changing drama of life escapes you. The many miles of scrub and underwood are diversified chiefly by crude advertisements. Here you are asked to purchase Duke's Mixture; there Castoria Toilet Powder is thrust upon your unwilling notice. In the few cities which you approach the frame-houses and plank-walks preserve the memory of the backwoods. In vain you look for the village church, which in Europe is never far away. In vain you look for the incidents which in our land lighten the tedium of a day's journey. All is barren and bleak monotony. The thin line of railway seems a hundred miles from the life of man. At one station I caught sight of an "Exposition Car," which bore the legend, "Cuba on Wheels," and I was surprised as at a miracle. Outside Niles, a little country town, a battered leather-covered shay was waiting to take wayfarers to the Michigan Inn; and the impression made by so simple a spectacle is the best proof of the railroad's isolation. There is but one interlude in the desolate expanse—Niagara.

Before he reaches the station called Niagara Falls, the tourist has a foretaste of what is in store for him. He is assailed in the train by touts, who would inveigle him into a hotel or let him a carriage, and to touts he is an unwilling prey so long as he remains within sight or hearing of the rapids. The trim little town which has grown up about the falls, and may be said to hang upon the water, has a holiday aspect. The sightseers, the little carriages, the summer-hotels, all wear the same garb of gaiety and leisure. There is a look of contented curiosity on the faces of all, who are not busy defacing the landscape with mills and power-stations, as of those about to contemplate a supreme wonder. And yet the sight of it brings the same sense of disappointment which the colossal masterpieces of nature always inspire. Not to be amazed at it would be absurd. To pretend to appreciate it is absurd also. "The Thunder of the Waters" can neither be painted upon canvas nor described in words. It is composed on a scale too large for human understanding. A giant might find some amusement in its friendly contemplation. A man can but stand aghast at its sound and size, as at some monstrous accident. He may compare the Fall on the American side with the Horse-shoe on the Canadian. He has no other standard of comparison, since Niagara not only transcends all other phenomena of its kind, but also our human vision and imagination. When you see the far-tossed spray lit up with a flash of iridescence, you catch at something which makes a definite impression; and you feel the same relief that a man may feel when he finds a friend in a mob of strangers. To heap up epithets upon this mysterious force is the idlest sport. Are you nearer to it when you have called it x "deliberate, vast, and fascinating"? You might as well measure its breadth and height, or estimate the number of gallons which descend daily from the broad swirling river above. A distinguished playwright once complained of Sophocles that he lacked human interest, and the charge may be brought with less injustice against Niagara. It is only through daring and danger that you can connect it with the human race; and you find yourself wondering where it was that Captain Webb was hurled to his death, or by what route the gallant little "Maid of the Mist" shot the rapids to escape the curiosity of the excise officer.

Nothing is more curious in the history of taste than the changed view which is taken to-day of natural scenery. Time was when the hand and mind of man were deemed necessary for a beautiful effect, A wild immensity of mountain or water was thought a mere form of ugliness; a garden was a waste if it were not trimmed to formality; and a savage moorland was fit only for the sheep to crop. The admiration of Father Hennepin, the companion of La Salle, and the first white man who ever gazed upon Niagara, was tempered by affright. "This wonderful Downfal," said he in 1678, "is compounded of Cross-streams of Water, and two Falls, with an Isle sloping along the middle of it. The Waters which fall from this horrible Precipice do foam and boyl after the most hideous manner imaginable, making an Outrageous Noise, more terrible than that of Thunder; for when the wind blows out of the South, their dismal roaring may be heard more than Fifteen Leagues off." These are the epithets of the seventeenth century,—"horrible," "hideous," "outrageous," "dismal." Now take the modern view, eloquently expressed in 1879 by the United States Commissioners, whose noble object was to preserve the Falls untouched for ever. "The value of Niagara to the world," they wrote, "and that which has obtained for it the homage of so many men whom the world reveres, lies in its power of appeal to the higher emotional and imaginative faculties, and this power is drawn from qualities and conditions too subtle to be known through verbal description. To a proper apprehension of these, something more than passing observation is necessary; to an enjoyment of them, something more than an instantaneous act of will." It is the old dispute between beauty and wonder, between classic and romantic. Who is in the right of it, the old priest or the modern commissioners? Each man will answer according to his temperament. For my part, I am on the side of Father Hennepin.

Niagara is not an inappropriate introduction to Chicago. For Chicago also is beyond the scale of human comprehension and endeavour. In mere size both are monstrous; it is in size alone that they are comparable. Long before he reaches "the grey city," as its inhabitants fondly call it, the traveller is prepared for the worst. At Pullman a thick pall already hangs over everything. The nearer the train approaches Chicago the drearier becomes the aspect. You are hauled through mile after mile of rubbish and scrap-heap. You receive an impression of sharp-edged flints and broken bottles. When you pass the "City Limits" you believe yourself at your journey's end. You have arrived only at the boundary of Chicago's ambition, and Chicago is forty minutes' distant. The station, which bears the name "102nd St.," is still in the prairies.

A little more patience and you catch a first glimpse of the lake—vast, smooth, and grey in the morning light. A jolt, and you are descending, grip in hand, upon the platform.

The first impression of Chicago, and the last, is of an unfinished monstrosity. It might be a vast railway station, built for men and women twenty feet high. The sky-scrapers, in which it cherishes an inordinate pride, shut out the few rays of sunlight which penetrate its dusky atmosphere. They have not the excuse of narrow space which their rivals in New York may plead. They are built in mere wantonness, for within the City Limits, whose distance from the centre is the best proof of Chicago's hopefulness, are many miles of waste ground, covered only with broken fences and battered shanties. And, as they raise their heads through the murky fog, these sky-scrapers wear a morose and sullen look. If they are not mere lumps, their ornament is hideously heavy and protrusive. They never combine, as they combine in New York, into an impressive whole. They clamour blatantly of their size, and that is all. And if the city be hideously aggressive, what word of excuse can be found for the outskirts, for the Italian and Chinese quarters, for the crude, new districts which fasten like limpets upon the formless mass of Chicago? These, to an enduring ugliness add a spice of cruelty and debauch, which are separate and of themselves.

In its suggestion of horror Chicago is democratic. The rich and the poor alike suffer from the prevailing lack of taste. The proud "residences" on the Lake Shore are no pleasanter to gaze upon than the sulky sky-scrapers. Some of them are prison-houses; others make a sad attempt at gaiety; all are amazingly unlike the dwelling-houses of men and women. Yet their owners are very wealthy. To them nothing is denied that money can buy, and it is thus that they prefer to express themselves and their ambitions. What, then, is tolerable in Chicago? Lincoln Park, which the smoke and fog of the city have not obscured, and the grandiose lake, whose fresh splendour no villainy of man can ever deface. And at one moment of the day, when a dark cloud hung over the lake, and the sun set in a red glory behind the sky-scrapers, each black, and blacker for its encircling smoke, Chicago rose superior to herself and her surroundings.

After ugliness, the worst foe of Chicago is dirt. A thick, black, sooty dust lies upon everything. It is at the peril of hands begrimed that you attempt to open a window. In the room that was allotted to me in a gigantic hotel I found a pair of ancient side-spring boots, once the property, no doubt, of a prominent citizen, and their apparition intensified the impression of uncleanness. The streets are as untidy as the houses; garbage is dumped in the unfinished roadways; and in or out of your hotel you will seek comfort in vain. The citizens of Chicago themselves are far too busy to think whether their city is spruce or untidy. Money is their quest, and it matters not in what circumstances they pursue it. The avid type is universal and insistent. The energy of New York is said to be mere leisure compared to the hustling of Chicago. Wherever you go you are conscious of the universal search after gold. The vestibule of the hotel is packed with people chattering, calculating, and telephoning. The clatter of the machine which registers the latest quotations never ceases. In the street every one is hurrying that he may not miss a lucrative bargain, until the industry and ambition of Chicago culminate in the Board of Trade.

The dial of the Board of Trade, or the Pit as it is called, is the magnet which attracts all the eyes of Chicago, for on its face is marked the shifting, changing price of wheat. And there on the floor, below the Strangers' Gallery, the gamblers of the West play for the fortunes and lives of men. They stand between the farmers, whose waving cornfields they have never seen, and the peasants of Europe, whose taste for bread they do not share. It is more keenly exciting to bet upon the future crop of wheat than upon the speed of a horse; and far larger sums may be hazarded in the Pit than on a racecourse. And so the livelong day the Bulls and Bears confront one another, gesticulating fiercely, and shouting at the top of their raucous voices. If on the one hand they ruin the farmer, or on the other starve the peasant, it matters not to them. They have enjoyed the excitement, and made perchance a vast fortune at another's expense. They are, indeed, the true parasites of commerce; and in spite of their intense voices and rapid gestures, there is an air of unreality about all their transactions. As I watched the fury of the combatants, I found myself wondering why samples of corn were thrown upon the floor. Perhaps they serve to feed the pigeons.

Materialism, then, is the frank end and aim of Chicago. Its citizens desire to get rich as quickly and easily as possible. The means are indifferent to them. It is the pace alone which is important. All they want is "a business proposition" and "found money." And when they are rich, they have no other desire than to grow richer. Their money is useless to them, except to breed more money. The inevitable result is a savagery of thought and habit. If we may believe the newspapers of Chicago, peaceful men of business are "held up" at noon in crowded streets. The revolver is still a potent instrument in this city of the backwoods. But savagery is never without its reaction. There has seldom been a community of barbarians which did not find relief in an extravagant sentimentality, and Chicago, in its hours of ease, is an enthusiastic patron of the higher life. As I have said, in culture it is fast outstripping Boston itself. It boasts more societies whose object is "the promotion of serious thought upon art, science, and literature" than any other city in the world. The clubs which it has established for the proper study of Ibsen and Browning are without number, It is as eager for the enlightenment of women as for sending up or down the price of corn. The craze, which is the mark of a crude society, will pass like many others, and, though it may appear sincere while it lasts, it is not characteristic. The one triumph of Chicago is its slang. It has invented a lingo more various and fuller of fancy than any known to man, and if it will forget Ibsen and exercise its invention after its own fashion, why should it not invent a new literature? Mr George Ade, the Shakespeare of Chicago, has already shown us what can be done with the new speech in his masterly 'Fables in Slang,' to read which is almost as good as a journey to the West; and there is no reason why he should not found a school.

Yet with all its faults and absurdities upon its face, Chicago is the happiest city in America. It is protected by the triple brass of pride against all the assaults of its enemies. Never in history was so sublime a vanity revealed; and it is hard for a stranger to understand upon what it is based. Chicago is Chicago—that is what its citizens say, with a flattered smile, which makes argument useless. Its dirt and dust do not disconcert its self-esteem. The oversized ugliness of its buildings are no disappointment to its candid soul, and if its peculiar virtue escape your observation, so much the worse for you. "The marvellous city of the West"—that is its own name, and it lives up to it without an effort. Its history, as composed by its own citizens, is one long paean of praise. One chronicler, to whose unconscious humour I am infinitely indebted, dedicates his work to "the children of Chicago, who, if the Lord spares them until they shall have attained the allotted span of life, will see this city the greatest metropolis on the globe." That is a modest estimate, and it makes us feel the inadequacy of our poor speech to hymn the glories of Chicago. And if you suggest a fault, its panegyrists are always ready with a counter-stroke. Having no taste for slaughter, I did not visit Packing Town, but, without admitting all the grave charges brought against Chicago's grandest industry, one might have supposed that the sudden translation of herds of cattle into potted meat was not unattended with some inconvenience. This suspicion, you are told, is an insult to the city. What might disgust the traveller elsewhere has no terrors in Chicago. "This Packing-Town odor," we are told by a zealot, "has been unjustly criticised. To any one accustomed to it there is only a pleasant suggestion of rich, ruddy blood and long rows of tempting 'sides' hung up to cool." I prefer not to be tempted. I can only bow before the ingenuity of this eulogy. And if, more seriously, you reproach the cynicism of the Pit, which on this side or that may compel ruin, you are met with a very easy rejoinder. "The Chicago Board of Trade"—it is the same apologist who speaks—"is a world-renowned commercial organisation. It exercises a wider and a more potential influence over the welfare of mankind than any other institution of its kind in existence." This assurance leaves you dumb. You might as well argue with a brass band as with a citizen of Chicago; and doubtless you would wave the flag yourself if you stayed long enough in the wonderful West.

But the panegyrist of the Pit, already quoted, helps us to explain Chicago's vanity. "The fortunes made and lost within the walls of the great building," says he proudly, "astonish the world." If Chicago can only astonish the world, that is enough. Its citizens fondly hope that everything they do is on the largest scale. Size, speed, and prominence are the three gods of their idolatry. They are not content until they—the citizens—are all prominent, and their buildings are all the largest that cumber the earth. It is a great comfort to those who gamble away their substance in the Board of Trade to reflect that the weathercock that surmounts its tower is the biggest ever seen by human eye. There is not one of them that will not tell you, with a satisfied smile, that the slowest of their fire-engines can go from one end of the city to the other in five seconds. There is not one of them who, in the dark recesses of his mind, is not sure that New York is a "back number." They are proud of the senseless height of their houses, and of the rapidity with which they mount towards the sky. They are proud of the shapeless towns which spring up about them like mushrooms in a single night. In brief, they are proud of all the things of which they should feel shame; and even when their buildings have been measured and their pace has been recognised, their vanity is still a puzzle. For, when all the world has been satisfactorily amazed, what boast is left to the citizens of Chicago? They cannot take delight in the soil, since the most of them do not belong to it. The patriotism of the cosmopolitan horde which is huddled together amid their lofty Cliffs must perforce be an artificial sentiment. They cannot look with satisfaction upon the dishevelled suburbs in which they live. They need not suppose the slaughtering of pigs and beeves is the highest duty of man.

But wherever they dwell and whatever they do, they are convinced of their own superiority. Their pride is not merely revealed in print; it is evident in a general familiarity of tone and manner. If your cabman wishes to know your destination, he prefaces his question with the immortal words, "Say, boys," and he thinks that he has put himself on amiable terms with you at once. Indeed, the newly-arrived stranger is instantly asked to understand that he belongs to a far meaner city than that in which he sojourns; and, even with the evidence of misapplied wealth before his eyes, he cannot believe it.

And what amiable visions do you carry away from Chicago besides the majesty of the lake, ever changing in colour and aspect, and the beauty of Lincoln Park? A single memory lingers in my mind. At sunset I saw a black regiment marching along Michigan Avenue, —marching like soldiers; and by its side on the pavement a laughing, shouting mob of negresses danced a triumphant cake-walk. They grinned and sang and chattered in perfect happiness and pride. They showed a frank pleasure in the prowess of their brothers and their friends. But, animated as the spectacle was, there was a sinister element in this joyous clatter. To an English eye it seemed a tragic farce—a veritable *danse macabre*.

Unhappy is the city which has no history; and what has Chicago to offer of history or tradition? What has it to tell the traveller? Once she was consumed, though she was not purified, by fire, and she still lives in the recollection. A visitor to a European city goes forth to admire a castle, a cathedral, a gallery of pictures. In Chicago he is asked to wonder at the shapeless residences of "prominent" citizens. And when the present civilisation fades and dies, what will be Chicago's ruins? Neither temple nor tower will be brought to the ground. There will be nothing to show the wandering New Zealander but a broken city, which was a scrap-heap before it was built; and the wandering New Zealander may be forgiven if he proclaim the uselessness of size and progress, if he ask how it has profited a city to buy and sell all the corn in the world, and in its destruction to leave not a wrack of comeliness behind.

NEW ENGLAND.

If in a country town we find an Inn called New, it is a sure sign of ancientry. The fresh and fragrant name survives the passing centuries. It clings to the falling house long after it has ceased to have an intelligible meaning. Taverns with a nobler sign and more arrogant aspect obscure its simpler merits. But there is a pride in its name, a dignity in its age, which a changing fashion will never destroy. And as it is with Inns, so it is with countries. New is an epithet redolent of antiquity. The province which once was, and is still called, New England, is very old America. It cannot be judged by the standards which are esteemed in New York or Chicago. The broad stream of what is called progress has left it undisturbed in its patient backwater. It recks as little of sky-scrapers as of transportation. Its towns are not ashamed of being villages, and the vanity which it guards is not the vanity of shapeless size, but the rarer vanity of a quiet and decent life.

No sooner does the English traveller leave Boston for the north than he enters what seems a familiar country. The towns which he passes, the rivers which he crosses, bear names, as I have said, to prove the faithful devotion the old adventurers felt for their native land. If they sought their fortune across the ocean, they piously preserved the memories of other days. Austere as were the early Puritans, bitterly as they smarted under what they supposed a political grievance, they did not regard the country of their origin with the fierce hatred which has sometimes inspired their descendants. The love of the New did not extinguish the love of the Old England. In Appledore and Portsmouth, in London and Manchester, in Newcastle and Dover, the ancient sentiment lives and breathes. And the New Englanders, once proud of their source, still cherish a pride in their blood, which they have kept pure from the contamination of the foreigner. Fortunately for itself, New England has fallen behind in the march of progress. There is nothing in its peaceful recesses to tempt the cosmopolitan horde which throngs the great cities of America. The hope of gain is there as small as the opportunity of gambling. A quiet folk, devoted to fishery and agriculture, is not worth plundering.

So it is there, if anywhere, that you may surprise the true-born American, and when you have surprised him, he very much resembles your own compatriot. His type and gesture are as familiar to you as his surroundings. Slow of speech and movement, he has not yet acquired the exhausting, purposeless love of speed which devours the more modern cities. He goes about his work with a perfect consciousness that there are four-and-twenty hours in the day. And as he is not the victim of an undue haste, he has leisure for a gracious civility. It is not for him to address a stranger with the familiarity characteristic of New York or Chicago. Though he know it not, and perhaps would resent it if he knew it, he is profoundly influenced by his origin. He has not lost the high seriousness, the quiet gravity, which distinguished his ancestors.

His towns, in aspect and sentiment, closely resemble himself. Portsmouth, for instance, which has not the same reason for self-consciousness as Salem or Concord, has retained the authentic features of the mother-land. You might easily match it in Kent or Essex. The open space in the centre of the town, the Athenæum—in style, name, and purpose, alike English—are of another age and country than their own. There is a look of trim elegance everywhere, which refreshes the eye; and over the streets there broods an immemorial peace, which even the echoing clangour of the Navy Yard cannot dispel. The houses, some of wood, built after the Colonial manner, others of red brick, and of a grave design, are in perfect harmony with their surroundings. Nothing is awry: nothing is out of place. And so severely consistent is the impression of age, that down on the sunlit quay, flanked by the lofty warehouses, the slope of whose roofs is masked by corbie-steps, you are surprised not to see riding at anchor the high-prowed galleons of the seventeenth century.

And, best of all, there is the quiet, simple Church of St John's, English in feeling as in origin. Though rebuilt a hundred years ago, on the site of an earlier church, it has remained loyal to its history, and is the true child of the eighteenth century. Is it not fitting that the communion-plate presented by Queen Caroline should be treasured here? That the sexton should still show you, even with a cold indifference, the stately prayer-books which once contained prayers for the king? That a bell, captured at Louisburg by Sir William Pepperell, should summon to the worship of God a people long forgetful of that proud achievement? Such are the evidences of an innate conservatism which has kept alive the old traditions of New England.

Thus for three hundred years Portsmouth has lived the happy life of a country town, and its historian sadly notes that until 1900 its population did not rise to 10,000. The historian need feel no regret: it is not by numbers that we may measure the stateliness of a city; and the dignity of Portsmouth is still plain for all to behold in the houses, to cite but two examples, of Governors Wentworth and Langdon, And then after this long spell of fortunate obscurity, Portsmouth became suddenly the centre of universal interest. By a curious irony this little, old-fashioned town was chosen to be the meeting-place of Russia and Japan, and the first experiment in modern diplomacy-was made in a place which has sacrificed nothing to a love of that intoxicant known as the spirit of the age. It was, in truth, a strange sight that Portsmouth saw a brief two years ago. Before its troubled eyes the stern conference of hostile nations was turned to comedy. A hundred and twenty eager reporters publicly put up their support for sale in exchange for information to the highest bidder. The representative of a great country was heard boasting to the gentlemen of the press of his own prowess. "The Japanese could not read in my face," said M. Witte, "what was passing in my heart." Isn't it wonderful? Would not the diplomatists of another age be ashamed of their *confrère* could they hear him brag of a rudimentary and long since dishonoured *finesse?* But the mere fact that M. Witte could make such a speech on American soil is a clear proof that the New World is not the proper field of diplomacy. The congresses of old were gay and secret. "Le congrès," said the Prince de Ligne at Vienna, "ne marche pas; il danse." It danced, and it kept inviolate the obligation of silence. The Congress at Portsmouth did not talk—it chattered; and it was an open injustice to the unbroken history of New England that President Roosevelt should have chosen this tranquil and ancient spot for a bold experiment in diplomacy by journalism.

Across the river lies Battery, even more remote from the world of greed and competition than Portsmouth. Here at last you discover what so often eludes you in America—the real countryside. The rough pleasant roads like English lanes, the beautiful wooden houses half hidden amid towering trees, and the gardens (or yards as they are called) not trim, like our English gardens, but of an unkempt beauty all their own,—these, with the memory of a gracious hospitality, will never fade from my mind. At Kittery, as at Portsmouth, you live in the past. There is nothing save an electric trolley and the motor engines of the fishing-boats to recall the bustle of to-day. Here is Fort M'Clary, a block-house built two centuries ago to stay the incursion of the Indians. There is the house of Pepperell, the hero of Lou-is-burg. Thus, rich in old associations, happy in its present seclusion, Kittery has a kind of personal charm, which is intensified by an obvious and striking contrast.

It was from Newport that I went to Kittery, and passed in a few hours from the modern to the ancient world. Not even New York gives a more vivid impression of the inappropriateness which is America's besetting sin, than Newport, whose gay inhabitants are determined, at all costs, to put themselves at variance with time and place. The mansions, called "cottages" in proud humility, are entirely out of proportion to their site and purpose. On the one hand you see a house as large as Chatsworth, bleak and treeless, with nothing to separate it from its ambitious neighbours but a wooden palisade. It suggests nothing so much as that it has lost its park, and mislaid its lodges. On the other, you see a massive pile, whose cas-tellated summit resembles nothing else than a county jail. And nowhere is there a possibility of ambush, nowhere a frail hint of secrecy. The people of Newport, moreover, is resolved to live up to its inappropriate environment. As it rejoices in the wrong kind of house, so it delights in the wrong sort of costume. The vain luxury of the place is expressed in a thousand strange antics. A new excitement is added to seabathing by the ladies, who face the waves in all the bravery of Parisian hats. To return unsullied from the encounter is a proof of the highest skill. Is it not better to preserve a deftly-poised hat from the mere contact of the waves than to be a tireless and intrepid swimmer?

Newport, in fact, has been haunted by a sort of ill-luck. It has never been able to make the best of itself. There was a time when its harbour bade fair to rival the harbour of New York, and when its inhabitants fondly believed that all the great ships of the world would find refuge under the splendid shadow of Rhode Island. And when this hope was disappointed for ever, Newport still possessed in herself all the elements of beauty. Whatever exquisite colour and perfect situation could give, was hers. What more can the eyes of man desire than green lawns and an incomparable sea? And there lies the old town to link the prosperity of to-day with the romance of yesterday. And there grow in wild profusion the scented hedges of honeysuckle and roses. And all of no avail. The early comers to Newport, it is true, understood that a real cottage of wood was in harmony with the place. They built their houses to the just scale of the landscape, and had they kept their own way how happy would have been the result! But beauty gave way to fashion; wealth usurped the sovereignty of taste; size was mistaken for grandeur, — in a word, the millionaire disfigured Newport to his whim.

And so it ceased to be a real place. It became a mere collection of opposing mansions and quarrelsome styles. If the vast "cottages," which raise their heads higher and higher in foolish rivalry, were swept away, no harm would be done. They are there by accident, and they will last only so long as a wayward fashion tolerates their presence. Battery, on the other hand, cannot be abolished by a caprice of taste. It is a village which has its roots in the past, and whose growth neither wealth nor progress has obscured. Above all, it possesses the virtue, great in towns as in men, of sincerity. It has not cut itself loose from its beginnings; its houses belong harmoniously to itself; and it has retained through two centuries the character of the old colonial days. Nor is it without an historical importance. Great names cling about it. The men of Battery fought on many a hard-won field against French and Indians, and, retired though it be from the broad stream of commerce and progress, it cannot dissipate the memory of loyal devotion to the crown and of military glory.

Its hero is Sir William Pepperell, soldier and merchant, whose thrift and prowess were alike remarkable. The son of a Tavistock fisherman, who pursued fortune in the New World with equal energy and success, he still further advanced his house in wealth and circumstance. Accustomed from boyhood to the dangers of Indian warfare, he was as apt for arms as for arts, and it is characteristic of the time and place that this prosperous merchant should be known to fame as the commander of a triumphant expedition. It was in 1745 that his chance came. For many years Louis-burg had afforded harbourage to French privateers, who had harried the coast of New England and captured rich cargoes of merchandise. At last Governor Shirley of Massachusetts resolved to attack it, and we may judge of the esteem in which Pepperell was held, by the fact that he was appointed to lead an expedition against a fortress deemed impregnable by the French, and known as the Dunkirk of America. His selection was a tribute not merely to his courage but to his tact. No man of his time was better fitted to control the conflicting tempers of the colonial militia, and he set forth at the head of his 4000 men under the best auspices. Being a Puritan in command of Puritans, he quickened the bravery of his comrades by a show of religious zeal. He made it plain that he was engaged in a war against papistry, and he asked George White-field, then in America, for a motto. "Nil desperandum, Christo duce," said the preacher; and thus heartened, the little fleet set sail on its triumphant journey. At first sight the contest seemed unequal. On one side was Duchambon, an experienced soldier, defending a fortress which had long been thought invincible. On the other was a plain merchant in command of no more than 4000 militiamen. But the very simplicity of Pepperell's attack ensured its success. He sailed into the harbour without warning and without fear, in the very eye of the French artillery, landed his men, and began a siege which resulted, after six weeks, in the reduction of Louisburg. It was a gallant feat of arms, marred only by the fact that a foolish Government declined to take advantage of a colonial victory. Three years later Louisburg was wickedly restored to France in exchange for certain advantages in India, and a foolish policy obscured for a while at least the eminent services of William Pepperell.

To-day the victor of Louisburg is not without fame—save in his own country. Fortunately for himself, Pepperell died before the War of the Revolution, and did not see the ruin which overtook his family. The property which had passed into the hands of his grandchildren was confiscated. They were guilty of loyalty to the crown and country for which their ancestor had fought, and the third generation was saved from the poorhouse "by the bounty of individuals on whom they had no claims for favour." In other words, Pepperell's memory was dishonoured, because in serving New England he had worn the king's uniform. In the eyes of the newly emancipated, treachery was retrospective. Pepperell's biographer explains his sin and its punishment with a perfect clarity. "The eventful life of Sir W. Pepperell," he writes, "closed a few years before the outbreak of the Revolution. Patriotism in his day implied loyalty and fidelity to the King of England; but how changed the meaning of that word in New England after the Declaration of Independence! Words and deeds before deemed patriotic were now traitorous, and so deeply was their moral turpitude impressed on the public mind as to have tainted popular opinions concerning the heroic deeds of our ancestors, performed in the King's service in the French Wars.... The War of the Revolution absorbed and neutralised all the heroic fame of the illustrious men that preceded, and the achievements of Pepperell, of Johnson, and of Bradstreet are now almost forgotten." These words were written in 1855, and they have not yet lost their truth.

For us this forgetfulness is not easily intelligible. It is our habit to attach ourselves closely to the past. If there have been conflicts, they have left no rancour, no bitterness. The winner has been modest, the loser magnanimous. The centuries of civil strife which devastated England imposed no lasting hostility. Nobody cares to-day whether his ancestor was Cavalier or Roundhead. The keenest Royalist is willing to acknowledge the noble prowess and the political genius of Cromwell. The hardiest Puritan pays an eager tribute to the exalted courage of Charles I. But the Americans have taken another view. They would, if they could, discard the bonds which unite them with England. For the mere glamour of independence they would sacrifice the glory of the past. They would even assume an hostility to their ancestors because these ancestors were of English blood. They seem to believe that if they forget their origin persistently enough it will be transformed. The top of their ambition would be reached if they could suppose that they were autochthonous,—that they sprang into being fully armed upon American soil. It irks them to think that other races have had a hand in creating "God's own country," and they are happiest when they can convince themselves that a man changes his heart and his mind as well as his sky when he leaves Europe for America. And so they pursue the policy of the ostrich. They bury the head of their past in the sandy desert of the present, and hope that nobody will detect the trick of their concealment.

In the Church of St John at Portsmouth there is, as I have said, an English prayer-book from which the page containing prayers for the king has been violently torn. This incident symbolises very aptly the attitude of America. The country has not yet recovered from the hostility which it once professed to George III. It assumes that a difference of policy always implies a moral taint. The American Colonies broke away from the mother country; therefore George III. was a knave, whose name may not be mentioned without dishonour, and all the brave men who served him in serving the colonies are dishonoured also. It is not quite clear why this feeling has been kept alive so long. Perhaps the violent rhetoric of the Declaration of Independence has aided its survival. Perhaps, too, the sense of gravity, which always overtakes the American public man when he considers what These States have achieved, is not without its weight. But whatever the cause, it is certain that shame and animosity still exist on the other side of the ocean: shame for noble deeds accomplished by brave men; animosity against a loyal antagonist, who long ago forgot the ancient quarrel and its consequence.

And yet the force and habit of tradition cannot forcibly be shaken off. Though New England, in forgetting the heroes who fought under British colours, has attempted to break the continuity of history, it is in New England where the links in the ancient chain are most stoutly coupled. Though all the prayer-books in the world be destroyed, the marks of its origin will still be stamped indelibly upon the face of the country. The very dourness which persuades these stern men to look with regret upon their beginnings is but a part of the puritanical character which drove them to take refuge in a foreign land. Stiff-necked and fanatical as they were, when they left England, they did but intensify their hard fanaticism in the new land. For there they were all of one party, and their children grew up without the wholesome stimulant of opposition. And if perchance one or two strayed from the fold of strict allegiance, the majority were cruel in punishment. They became persecutors for what they believed was righteousness' sake, and their cruelty was the more severe because it was based, as they believed, upon a superior morality. And so they grew, as an American historian has said, to hate the toleration for which they once fought, to deplore the liberty of conscience for whose sake they had been ready to face exile. What in themselves they praised for liberty and toleration, they denounced in others as carelessness or heresy. So they cultivated a hard habit of thought; so they esteemed too seriously the efforts they made in the cause of freedom; so they still exaggerate the importance of the Revolution, which the passage of time should compel them to regard with a cold and dispassionate eye.

But if in a certain pitilessness of character the New Englanders are more English than the English, they still resemble the Puritans of the seventeenth century in their love of a well-ordered life. It was in their towns and villages that the old colonial life flourished to the wisest purpose. The houses which they built, and which still stand, are the perfection of elegance and comfort. The simplicity of their aspect is matched by the beauty which confronts you when once you have crossed the threshold. The columns which flank the porch, the pilasters which break the monotony of the wooden walls, are but a faint indication of the elegance within. Like the palaces of the Moors, they reserve the best of themselves for the interior, and reveal all their beauty only to their intimates. The light staircases, with turned rails and lyre-shaped ends; the panelled rooms; the dainty fireplaces, adorned with Dutch tiles; the English furniture, which has not left its first home; the spacious apartments, of which the outside gives no warning, — these impart a quiet dignity, a pleasant refinement, to the colonial houses which no distance of time or space can impair. There is a house at Kittery of which the planks were cut out there in the forest, were sent to England to be carved and shaped, and were then returned to their native woodland to be fashioned into a house. Thus it belongs to two worlds, and thus it is emblematic of the New Englanders who dwell about it, and who, owing their allegiance to a new country, yet retain the impress of a character which was their ancestors' almost three centuries ago.

THE YELLOW PRESS.

If all countries may boast the Press which they deserve, America's desert is small indeed. No civilised country in the world has been content with newspapers so grossly contemptible as those which are read from New York to the Pacific Coast. The journals known as Yellow would be a disgrace to dusky Timbuctoo, and it is difficult to understand the state of mind which can tolerate them. Divorced completely from the world of truth and intelligence, they present nothing which an educated man would desire to read. They are said to be excluded from clubs and from respectable houses. But even if this prohibition be a fact, their proprietors need feel no regret. We are informed by the Yellowest of Editors that his burning words are read every day by five million men and women.

What, then, is the aspect and character of these Yellow Journals? As they are happily strange on our side the ocean, they need some description. They are ill-printed, over-illustrated sheets, whose end and aim are to inflame a jaded or insensitive palate. They seem to address the blind eye and the sluggish mind of the halfwitted. The wholly unimportant information which they desire to impart is not conveyed in type of the ordinary shape and size. The "scare" headlines are set forth in letters three inches in height. It is as though the editors of these sheets are determined to exhaust your attention. They are not content to tell you that this or that inapposite event has taken place. They pant, they shriek, they yell. Their method represents the beating of a thousand big drums, the blare of unnumbered trumpets, the shouted blasphemies of a million raucous throats. And if, with all this noise dinning in your ear, you are persuaded to read a Yellow sheet, which is commonly pink in colour, you are grievously disappointed. The thing is not even sensational. Its "scare" headlines do but arouse a curiosity which the "brightest and brainiest" reporter in the United States is not able to satisfy.

Of what happens in the great world you will find not a trace in the Yellow Journals. They betray no interest in politics, in literature, or in the fine arts. There is nothing of grave importance which can be converted into a "good story." That a great man should perform a great task is immaterial. Noble deeds make no scandal, and are therefore not worth reporting. But if you can discover that the great man has a hidden vice, or an eccentric taste in boots or hats, there is "copy" ready to your hand. All things and all men must be reduced to a dead level of imbecility. The Yellow Press is not obscene—it has not the courage for that. Its proud boast is that it never prints a line that a father might not read to his daughter. It is merely personal and impertinent. No one's life is secure from its spies. No privacy is sacred. Mr Stead's famous ideal of an ear at every keyhole is magnificently realised in America. A hundred reporters are ready, at a moment's notice, to invade houses, to uncover secrets, to molest honest citizens with indiscreet questions. And if their victims are unwilling to respond, they pay for it with public insult and malicious invention. Those who will not bow to the common tyrant of the Press cannot complain if words are ascribed to them which they never uttered, if they are held guilty of deeds from which they would shrink in horror. Law and custom are alike powerless to fight this tyranny, which is the most ingenious and irksome form of blackmail yet invented.

The perfect newspaper, if such were possible, would present to its readers a succinct history of each day as it passes. It would weigh with a scrupulous hand the relative importance of events. It would give to each department of human activity no more than its just space. It would reduce scandal within the narrow limits which ought to confine it. Under its wise auspices murder, burglary, and suicide would be deposed from the eminence upon which an idle curiosity has placed them. Those strange beings known as public men would be famous not for what their wives wear at somebody else's "At Home," but for their own virtues and attainments. The foolish actors and actresses, who now believe themselves the masters of the world, would slink away into *entrefilets* on a back page. The perfect newspaper, in brief, would resemble a Palace of Truth, in which deceit was impossible and vanity ridiculous. It would crush the hankerers after false reputations, it would hurl the foolish from the mighty seats which they try to fill, and it would present an invaluable record to future generations.

What picture of its world does the Yellow Press present? A picture of colossal folly and unpardonable indiscretion. If there be a museum which preserves these screaming sheets, this is the sort of stuff which in two thousand years will puzzle the scholars: "Mrs Jones won't admit Wedding," "Millionaires Bet on a Snake Fight," "Chicago Church Girl Accuses Millionaire," "Athletics make John D. forget his Money." These are a few pearls hastily strung together, and they show what jewels of intelligence are most highly prized by the Greatest Democracy on earth. Now and again the editor takes his readers into his confidence and asks them to interfere in the affairs of persons whom they will never know. Here, for instance, is a characteristic problem set by an editor whose knowledge of his public exceeds his respect for the decencies of life: "What Mrs Washington ought to do. Her husband Wall Street Broker. Got tired of Her and Deserted. But Mrs Washington, who still loves him dearly, Is determined to win him back. And here is the Advice of the Readers of this Journal." Is it not monstrous—this interference with the privacy of common citizens? And yet this specimen has an air of dignity compared with the grosser exploits of the hired eavesdropper. Not long since there appeared in a Sunday paper a full list, with portraits and biographies, of all the ladies in New York who are habitual drunkards. From which it is clear that the law of libel has sunk into oblivion, and that the cowhide is no longer a useful weapon.

The disastrous effect upon the people of such a Press as I have described is obvious. It excites the nerves of the feeble, it presents a hideously false standard of life, it suggests that nobody is secure from the omnipotent eavesdropper, and it preaches day after day at the top of its husky voice the gospel of snobbishness. But it is not merely the public manners which it degrades; it does its best to hamper the proper administration of the law. In America trial by journalism has long supplemented, and goes far to supplant, trial by jury. If a murder be committed its detection is not left to the officers of the police. A thousand reporters, cunning as monkeys, active as sleuth-hounds, are on the track. Whether it is the criminal that they pursue or an innocent man is indifferent to them. Heedless of injustice, they go in search of "copy." They interrogate the friends of the victim, and they uncover the secrets of all the friends and relatives he may have possessed. They care not how they prejudice the public mind, or what wrong they do to innocent men. If they make a fair trial impossible, it matters not. They have given their tired readers a new sensation; they have stimulated gossip in a thousand tenement houses; justice may fall in ruins so long as they sell another edition. And nobody protests against their unbridled licence, not even when they have made it an affair of the utmost difficulty and many weeks to empanel an unprejudiced jury.

The greatest opportunity of the Yellow Press came when a Mr H. K. Thaw murdered an accomplished architect. The day after the murder the trial began in the newspapers, and it was "run as a serial" for months. The lives of the murderer and his victim were uncovered with the utmost effrontery. The character of the dead man was painted in the blackest colours by cowards, who knew that they were beyond the reach of vengeance. The murderer's friends and kinsmen were compelled to pay their tribute to the demon of publicity. The people was presented with plans of the cell in which the man Thaw was imprisoned, while photographs of his wife and his mother were printed day after day that a silly mob might note the effect of anguish on the human countenance. And, not content with thus adorning the tale, the journals were eloquent in pointing the moral. Sentimental spinsters were invited to warn the lady typewriters of America that death and ruin inevitably overtake the wrongdoer. Stern-eyed clergymen thought well to anticipate justice in sermons addressed to erring youth. Finally, *a plébiscite* decided, by 2 to 1, that Thaw should immediately be set free. And when you remember the arrogant tyranny of the Yellow Journals, you are surprised that at the mere sound of the people's voice the prison doors did not instantly fly open.

We have been told, as though it were no more than a simple truth, that the Yellow Press—the journals owned by Mr Hearst—not merely made the Spanish-American War, but procured the assassination of Mr M'Kinley. The statement seems incredible, because it is difficult to believe that such stuff as this should have any influence either for good or evil. The idle gossip and flagrant scandal which are its daily food do not appear to be efficient leaders of opinion. But it is the Editorial columns which do the work of conviction, and they assume an air of gravity which may easily deceive the unwary. And their gravity is the natural accompaniment of scandal. There is but a slender difference between barbarity and senti-mentalism. The same temper which delights in reading of murder and sudden death weeps with anguish at the mere hint of oppression. No cheek is so easily bedewed by the unnecessary tear as the cheek of the ruffian—and those who compose the "editorials" for Mr Hearst's papers have cynically realised this truth. They rant and they cant and they argue, as though nothing but noble thoughts were permitted to lodge within the poor brains of their readers. Their favourite gospel is the gospel of Socialism. They tell the workers that the world is their inalienable inheritance, that skill and capital are the snares of the evil one, and that nothing is worth a reward save manual toil. They pretend for a moment to look with a kindly eye upon the Trusts, because, when all enterprises and industries are collected into a small compass, the people will have less trouble in laying hands upon them. In brief, they teach the supreme duty of plunder with all the *staccato* eloquence at their command. For the man whose thrift and energy have helped him to success they have nothing but contempt. They cannot think of the criminal without bursting into tears. And, while they lay upon the rich man the guilty burden of his wealth, they charge the community with the full responsibility for the convict's misfortune. Such doctrines, cunningly taught, and read day after day by the degenerate and unrestrained, can only have one effect, and that effect, no doubt, the "editorials" of the Yellow Press will some day succeed in producing.

The result is, of course, revolution, and revolution is being carefully and insidiously prepared after the common fashion. Not a word is left unsaid that can flatter the criminal or encourage the thriftless. Those who are too idle to work but not too idle to read the Sunday papers are told that it will be the fault of their own inaction, not of the Yellow Press, if they do not some day lay violent hands upon the country's wealth. And when they are tired of politics the Yellow Editors turn to popular philosophy or cheap theology for the solace of their public. To men and women excited by the details of the last murder they discourse of the existence of God in short, crisp sentences, — and I know not which is worse, the triviality of the discourse or its inappositeness. They preface one of their most impassioned exhortations with the words: "If you read this, you will probably think you have wasted time." Though this might with propriety stand for the motto of all the columns of all Mr Hearst's journals, here it is clearly used in the same hope which inspires the sandwichman to carry on his front the classic legend: "Please do not look on my back." But what is dearest to the souls of these editors is a mean commonplace. One leader, which surely had a triumphant success, is headed, "What the Bar-tender Sees." And the exordium is worthy so profound a speculation. "Did you ever stop to think," murmurs the Yellow philosopher, "of all the strange beings that pass before him?" There's profundity for you! There's invention! Is it wonderful that five million men and women read these golden words, or others of a like currency, every day?

And politics, theology, and philosophy are all served up in the same thick sauce of sentiment. The "baby" seems to play a great part in the Yellow morality. One day you are told, "A baby can educate a man"; on another you read, "Last week's baby will surely talk some day," and you are amazed, as at a brilliant discovery. And you cannot but ask: To whom are these exhortations addressed? To children or to idiots? The grown men and women of the United States, can hardly regard such poor twaddle as this with a serious eye. And what of the writers? How can they reconcile their lofty tone, which truly is above suspicion, with the shameful sensationalism of their news-columns? They know not the meaning of sincerity. If they really believed that "a baby can educate a man," they would suppress their reporters. In short, they are either blind or cynical. From these alternatives there is no escape, and for their sakes, as well as for America's, I hope they write with their tongue in their cheeks.

The style of the Yellow Journals is appropriate to their matter. The headlines live on and by the historic present; the text is as bald as a paper of statistics. It is the big type that does the execution. The "story" itself, to use the slang of the newspaper, is seldom either humorous or picturesque. Bare facts and vulgar incidents are enough for the public, which cares as little for wit as for sane writing. One fact only can explain the imbecility of the Yellow Press: it is written for immigrants, who have but an imperfect knowledge of English, who prefer to see their news rather than to read it, and who, if they must read, can best understand words of one syllable and sentences of no more than five words.

For good or evil, America has the sole claim to the invention of the Yellow Press. It came, fully armed, from the head of its first proprietor, It owes nothing to Europe, nothing to the traditions of its own country. It grew out of nothing, and, let us hope, it will soon disappear into nothingness. The real Press of America was rather red than yellow. It had an energy and a character which still exist in some more reputable sheets, and which are the direct antithesis of Yellow sensationalism. The horsewhip and revolver were as necessary to its conduct as the pen and inkpot. If the editors of an older and wiser time insulted their enemies, they were ready to defend themselves, like men. They did not eavesdrop and betray. They would have scorned to reveal the secrets of private citizens, even though they did not refrain their hand from their rivals. Yet, with all their brutality, they were brave and honourable, and you cannot justly measure the degradation of the Yellow Press unless you cast your mind a little further back and contemplate the achievement of another generation.

The tradition of journalism came to America from England. 'The Sun,' 'The Tribune,' and 'The Post,' as wise and trustworthy papers as may be found on the surface of the globe, are still conscious of their origin, though they possess added virtues of their own. 'The New York Herald,' as conducted by James Gordon Bennett the First, modelled its scurrilous energy upon the Press of our eighteenth century. The influence of Junius and the pamphleteers was discernible in its columns, and many of its articles might have been signed by Wilkes himself. But there was something in 'The Herald' which you would seek in vain in Perry's 'Morning Chronicle,' say, or 'The North Briton,' and that was the free-and-easy style of the backwoods. Gordon Bennett grasped as well as any one the value of news. He boarded vessels far out at sea that he might forestall his rivals. In some respects he was as "yellow" as his successor, whose great exploit of employing a man convicted of murder to report the trial of a murderer is not likely to be forgotten. On the other hand, he set before New York the history of Europe and of European thought with appreciation and exactitude. He knew the theatre of England and France more intimately than most of his contemporaries, and he did a great deal to encourage the art of acting in his own country. Above all things he was a fighter, both with pen and fist. He had something of the spirit which in-spired the old mining-camp. "We never saw the man we feared," he once said, "nor the woman we had not some liking for." That healthy, if primitive, sentiment breathes in all his works. And his magnanimity was equal to his courage. "I have no objection to forgive enemies," he wrote, "particularly after I have trampled them under my feet." This principle guided his life and his journal, and, while it gave a superb dash of energy to his style, it put a wholesome fear into the hearts and heads of his antagonists.

One antagonist there was who knew neither fear nor forgetfulness, and he attacked Bennett again and again. Bennett returned his blows, and then made most admirable "copy" of the assault. The last encounter between the two is so plainly characteristic of Bennett's style that I quote his description in his own words. "As I was leisurely pursuing my business yesterday in Wall Street," wrote Bennett, "collecting the information which is daily disseminated in 'The Herald,' James Watson Webb came up to me, on the northern side of the street—said something which I could not hear distinctly, then pushed me down the stone steps leading to one of the brokers' offices, and commenced fighting with a species of brutal and demoniac desperation characteristic of a fury. My damage is a scratch, about three-quarters of an inch in length, on the third finger of the left hand, which I received from the iron railing I was forced against, and three buttons torn from my vest, which my tailor will reinstate for six cents. His loss is a rent from top to bottom of a very beautiful black coat, which cost the ruffian $40, and a blow in the face which may have knocked down his throat some of his infernal teeth for all I know. Balance in my favour $39.94. As to intimidating me, or changing my course, the thing cannot be done. Neither Webb nor any other man shall, or can, intimidate me…. I may be attacked, I may be assailed, I may be killed, I may be murdered, but I will never succumb."

There speaks the true Gordon Bennett, and his voice, though it may be the voice of a ruffian, is also the voice of a man who is certainly courageous and is not without humour. It is not from such a tradition as that, that the Yellow Press emerged. It does not want much pluck to hang about and sneak secrets. It is the pure negation of humour to preach Socialism in the name of the criminal and degenerate. To judge America by this product would be monstrously unfair, but it corresponds perforce to some baser quality in the cosmopolitans of the United States, and it cannot be overlooked. As it stands, it is the heaviest indictment of the popular taste that can be made. There is no vice so mean as impertinent curiosity, and it is upon this curiosity that the Yellow Press meanly lives and meanly thrives.

What is the remedy? There is none, unless time brings with it a natural reaction. It is as desperate a task to touch the Press as to change the Constitution. The odds against reform are too great. A law to check the exuberance of newspapers would never survive the attacks of the newspapers themselves.

Nor is it only in America that reform is necessary. The Press of Europe, also, has strayed so far from its origins as to be a danger to the State. In their inception the newspapers were given freedom, that they might expose and check the corruption and dishonesty of politicians. It was thought that publicity was the best cure for intrigue. For a while the liberty of the Press seemed justified. It is justified no longer. The licence which it assumes has led to far worse evils than those which it was designed to prevent. In other words, the slave has become a tyrant, and where is the statesman who shall rid us of this tyranny? Failure alone can kill what lives only upon popular success, and it is the old-fashioned, self-respecting journals which are facing ruin. Prosperity is with the large circulations, and a large circulation is no test of merit. Success is made neither by honesty nor wisdom. The people will buy what flatters its vanity or appeals to its folly. And the Yellow Press will flourish, with its headlines and its vulgarity, until the mixed population of America has sufficiently mastered the art of life and the English tongue to demand something better wherewith to solace its leisure than scandal and imbecility.

LIBERTY AND PATRIOTISM.

Guarding the entrance to New York there stands, lofty and austere, the statue of Liberty. It is this statue which immigrants, on their way to Ellis Island, are wont to apostrophise. To contemplate it is, we are told, to know the true meaning of life, to taste for the first time the sweets of an untrammelled freedom. No sooner does M. Bartholdi's beneficent matron smile upon you, than you cast off the chains of an ancient slavery. You forget in a moment the years which you have misspent under the intolerable burden of a monarch. Be you Pole or Russ, Briton or Ruthenian, you rejoice at the mere sight of this marvel, in a new hope, in a boundless ambition. Unconscious of what awaits you, you surrender yourself so eagerly to the sway of sentiment that you are unable to observe the perfections of your idol. You see only its vast size. You are content to believe the official statement that 305 feet separate the tip of the lady's torch from low water. You know that you gaze on the largest statue upon earth. And surely it should be the largest, for it symbolises a greater mass of Liberty than ever before was gathered together upon one continent.

For Liberty is a thing which no one in America can escape. The old inhabitant smiles with satisfaction as he murmurs the familiar word. At every turn it is clubbed into the unsuspecting visitor. If an aspirant to the citizenship of the Republic declined to be free, he would doubtless be thrown into a dungeon, fettered and manacled, until he consented to accept the precious boon. You cannot pick up a newspaper without being reminded that Liberty is the exclusive possession of the United States. The word, if not the quality, is the commonplace of American history. It looks out upon you—the word again, not the quality—from every hoarding. It is uttered in every discourse, and though it irks you to listen to the boasting of "Liberty", as it irks you when a man vaunts his honour, you cannot but inquire what is this fetish which distinguishes America from the rest of the habitable globe, and what does it achieve for those who worship it.

In what, then, does the Liberty of America consist? Is it in freedom of opportunity? A career is open to all the talents everywhere. The superstitions of Europe, the old-fashioned titles of effete aristocracies, are walls more easily surmounted than the golden barricades of omnipotent corporations. Does it consist in political freedom? If we are to believe in the pedantry that Liberty is the child of the ballot-box, then America has no monopoly of its blessings. The privilege of voting is almost universal, and the freedom which this poor privilege confers is within the reach of Englishman, German, or Frenchman. Indeed, it is America which sets the worst stumbling-block in the voter's path. The citizen, however high his aspiration after Liberty may be, wages a vain warfare against the cunning of the machine. Where repeaters and fraudulent ballots flourish, it is idle to boast the blessings of the suffrage. Such institutions as Tammany are essentially practical, but they do not help the sacred cause commemorated in M. Bartholdi's statue; and if we would discover the Liberty of America, we must surely look outside the ring of boodlers and politicians who have held the franchise up to ridicule. Is, then, the boasted Liberty a liberty of life? One comes and goes with ease as great in England as in America. There are even certain restrictions imposed in the home of Freedom, of which we know nothing on this side the Atlantic, where we fear the curiosity of the Press as little as we dread the exactions of hungry monopolies. Of many examples, two will suffice to illustrate the hardships of a democratic tyranny. Not long since the most famous actress of our generation was prevented by a trust of all-powerful managers from playing in the theatres of America, and was compelled to take refuge in booths and tents. Being a lady of courage and resource, she filled her new *rôle* with perfect success, and completely outwitted her envious rivals. The victory was snatched, by the actress's own energy, from the very jaws of Liberty. Far more unfortunate was the fate of M. Gorki, who visited America to preach the gospel of Freedom, as he thought, in willing ears. With the utmost propriety he did all that was expected of him. He apostrophised the statue in a voice tremulous with emotion. He addressed the great Continent, as it loves to be addressed. "America! America!" he exclaimed, "how I have longed for this day, when my foot should tread the soil where despotism cannot live!" Alas for his lost enthusiasm!

A despot, grim and pitiless, was waiting for him round the corner. In other words, the proprietor of his hotel discovered that Mme. Gorki had no right to that name, and amid the cheers of the guests he and his companion were driven shamefully into the street. Were it not for the wanton inconvenience inflicted upon M. Gorki, the comedy of the situation would be priceless. The Friends of Russian Freedom, piously enamoured of assassination, and listening intently for the exquisite reverberation of the deadly bomb, sternly demand of the Apostle his marriage-lines. The Apostle of Revolution, unable to satisfy the demand, is solemnly excommunicated, as if he had apostrophised no statue, as if he had felt no expansion of his lungs, no tingling of his blood, when he first breathed the air of Freedom. O Liberty! Liberty! many follies have been committed in thy name! And now thy voice is hushed in inextinguishable laughter!

The truth is, American Liberty is the mere creature of rhetoric. It is a survival from the time when the natural rights of man inspired a simple faith, when eager citizens declared that kings were the eternal enemies of Freedom. Its only begetter was Thomas Jefferson, and its gospel is preached in the famous Declaration of Independence. The dogmatism and pedantry upon which it is based are easily confuted. Something else than a form of government is necessary to ensure political and personal liberty. Otherwise the Black Republic would be a model to England. But Jefferson, not being a philosopher, and knowing not the rudiments of history, was unable to look beyond the few moral maxims which he had committed to memory. He was sure that the worst republic was better than the noblest tyranny the world had ever seen. He appealed not to experience but to sentiment, and he travelled up and down Europe with his eyes closed and his mind responsive only to the echoes of a vain theory. "If all the evils which can arise among us," said he, "from the republican form of our government, from this day to the Day of Judgment, could be put into a scale against what France suffers from its monarchical form in a week, or England in a month, the latter would preponderate." Thus he said, in sublime ignorance of the past, in perfect misunderstanding of the future. And his empty words echo to-day in the wigwams of Tammany.

All forms of government have their strength and their weakness. They are not equally suitable to all races and to all circumstances. It was this obvious truth that Jefferson tore to shreds before the eyes of his compatriots. He persuaded them to accept his vague generalities as a sober statement of philosophic truth, and he aroused a hatred of kingship in America which was comic in expression and disastrous in result. It was due to his influence that plain citizens hymned the glories of "Guillotina, the Tenth Muse," and fell down in worship before a Phrygian cap. It was due to his influence that in 1793 the death of Louis XVI. was celebrated throughout the American continent with grotesque symbolism and farcical solemnity. A single instance is enough to prove the malign effect of Jefferson's teaching. At Philadelphia the head of a pig was severed from its body, and saluted as an emblem of the murdered king.

"Each one," says the historian, "placing the cap of liberty upon his head, pronounced the word 'tyrant'! and proceeded to mangle with his knife the head of the luckless creature doomed to be served for so unworthy a company." And the voice of Jefferson still speaks in the land. Obedient to his dictate, Americans still take a sentimental view of Liberty. For them Liberty is still an emotion to feel, not a privilege to enjoy. They are willing to believe that a monarch means slavery. America is the greatest republic on earth, they argue, and therefore it is the chosen and solitary home of Freedom.

So, ignoring the peculiar enslavements of democracy, forgetting the temptations to which the noblest republic is exposed, they proclaim a monopoly of the sovereign virtue, and cast a cold eye of disdain upon the tradition of older countries. The author of 'Triumphant Democracy,' for instance, asserts that he "was denied political equality by his native land." We do not know for what offence he was thus heavily punished, and it is consoling to reflect that the beloved Republic has made him "the peer of any man." It has not made any other man his peer. He is separated far more widely by his wealth from the workmen, whom he patronises, than the meanest day-labourer in England from the dukes to whom he is supposed to bend the knee; and if Mr Carnegie's be the fine flower of American Liberty, we need hardly regret that ours is of another kind.

In Jefferson's despite, men are not made free and equal by the frequent repetition of catchwords, and it is by a fine irony that America, which prides itself upon a modern spirit, should still be swayed by a foolish superstition, more than a century old, that the cant of Liberty and Equality, uttered by a slave-owner in 1776, should still warp its intelligence. "I don't know what liberty means," said Lord Byron, "never having seen it;" and it was in candour rather than in experience that Byron differed from his fellows. Nor has any one else seen what eluded Byron. A perfectly free man must be either uncivilised or decivilised—a savage stronger than his fellows or an undetected anarch armed with a bomb, A free society is a plain contradiction, for a society must be controlled by law, and law is an instant curtailment of Liberty. And, if you would pursue this chimera, it is not in a democracy that you are likely to surprise it. Liberty is a prize which will always escape you in a mob. The supremacy of the people means the absolute rule of the majority, in deference to which the mere citizen must lay aside all hope of independence. In life, as in politics, a democratic minority has no rights. It cannot set its own pace; it cannot choose its own route; it must follow the will of others, not its own desire; and it is small comfort to the slave, whose chains gall him, that the slave-driver bears the name of a free man.

Liberty, in brief, is a private, not a public, virtue. It has naught to do with extended franchises or forms of government. The free man may thrive as easily under a tyranny as in a republic. Is it not true Liberty to live in accord with one's temperament or talent? And as the best laws cannot help this enterprise, so the worst cannot hinder it. You will discover Liberty in Russia as in America, in England as in France,—everywhere, indeed, where men refuse to accept the superstitions and doctrines of the mob. But the Americans are not content to possess the Liberty which satisfies the rest of the world. With characteristic optimism they boast the possession of a rare and curious quality. In Europe we strive after Freedom in all humility of spirit, as after a happy state of mind. In America they advertise it—like a patent medicine.

America's view of Patriotism is distinguished by the same ingenious exaggeration as her view of Liberty. She has as little doubt of her Grandeur as of her Freedom. She is, in brief, "God's own country," and in her esteem Columbus was no mere earthly explorer; he was the authentic discoverer of the Promised Land. Neither argument nor experience will ever shake the American's confidence in his noble destiny. On all other questions uncertainty is possible. It is not possible to discuss America's supremacy. In arms as in arts, the United States are unrivalled. They alone enjoy the blessings of civilisation. They alone have been permitted to combine material with moral progress. They alone have solved the intricate problems of life and politics. They have the biggest houses, the best government, and the purest law that the world has ever known. Their universities surpass Oxford and Cambridge, Paris and Leipzig, in learning, as their Churches surpass the Churches of the old world in the proper understanding of theology. In brief, to use their own phrase, America is "It," the sole home of the good and great.

Patriotism such as this, quick in enthusiasm, simple in faith, may prove, if properly handled, a national asset of immeasurable value. And in public the Americans admit no doubt. Though they do not hesitate to condemn the boodlers who prey upon their cities, though they deplore the corrupt practices of their elections, they count all these abuses as but spots upon a brilliant sun. A knowledge of his country's political dishonesty does not depress the true patriot. He is content to think that his ideals are as lofty as their realisation is remote, and that the triumph of graft is as nothing compared with a noble sentiment. The result is that the Americans refuse to weaken their national prestige by the advertised cannibalism which is so popular in England. They are for their country, right or wrong. They do not understand the anti-patriot argument, which was born of the false philosophy of the eighteenth century, and which has left so evil a mark upon our political life. To them the phenomenon which we call Pro-Boerism is not easily intelligible. They take an open pride in their country and their flag, and it seems certain that, when they stand in the presence of an enemy, they will not weaken their national cause by dissension.

This exultant Patriotism is the more remarkable when we reflect upon what it is based. The love of country, as understood in Europe, depends upon identity of race, upon community of history and tradition. It should not be difficult for those whose fathers have lived under the same sky, and breathed the same air, to sacrifice their prosperity or their lives to the profit of the State. In making such a sacrifice they are but repaying the debt of nurture. To the vast majority of Americans this sentiment, grafted on the past, can make no appeal. The only link which binds them to America is their sudden arrival on alien soil. They are akin to the Anglo-Saxons, who first peopled the continent, neither in blood nor in sympathy. They carry with them their national habits and their national tastes. They remain Irish, or German, or Italian, with a difference, though they bear the burden of another State, and assume the privileges of another citizenship. But there is no mistake about their Patriotism. Perhaps those shout loudest who see the Star-spangled Banner unfurled for the first time, and we are confronted in America with the outspoken expression of a sentiment which cannot be paralleled elsewhere on the face of the globe.

They tread the same ground, these vast hordes of patriots, they obey the same laws,—that is all. Are they, then, moved by a spirit of gratitude, or do they feel the same loyalty which animates a hastily gathered football team, which plays not for its honour but for the profit of its manager? Who shall say? One thing only is certain: the Patriotism of the cosmopolites, if it be doubtful in origin, is by no means doubtful in expression. On every Fourth of July the Americans are free to display the love of their Country, and they use this freedom without restraint. From the Atlantic to the Pacific Coast, from Vermont to Mexico, the Eagle screams aloud. She screams from early morn to dewy eve. And there is nothing to silence her screaming save the explosion of innumerable crackers, the firing of countless pistols.

For this day the youth of America is given full licence to shoot his inoffensive neighbours, and, if he will, to commit the happy despatch upon him-self. The next morning the newspapers chronicle the injuries which have been inflicted on and by the boys of New York, for the most part distinguished by foreign names, with the cold accuracy bred of long habit. And while the boys prove their patriotism by the explosion of crackers, their fathers, with equal enthusiasm, devote themselves to the waving of flags. They hold flags in their hands, they carry them in their buttonholes, they stick them in their hats, they wear them behind their ears. Wherever your eye is cast, there are flags to dazzle it, flags large and flags small, an unbroken orgie of stars and stripes. It is, in fact, the Guy Fawkes Day of America. And who is the Guy? None other than George III. of blessed memory. For the Fourth of July has its duties as well as its pleasures, and the chief of its duties is the public reading of the Declaration of Independence. In every town and hamlet Jefferson's burning words are proclaimed in the ears of enthusiastic citizens. It is pointed out to a motley crowd of newly arrived immigrants that George, our king, of whom they had not heard yesterday, was unfit to be the ruler of a free people. And lest the inestimable benefit of Jefferson's eloquence should be lost to one single suddenly imported American, his declaration is translated into Yiddish for the benefit of those to whom English is still an unknown tongue. In a voice trembling with emotion, the orator assures the starving ill-clad Pole and the emaciated Bohemian that all men are free and equal; and so fine is the air of the Great Republic that this proposition, which refutes itself, is firmly believed for the moment by the penniless and hungry. And when the sun sets, and darkness enwraps the happy land, fireworks put a proper finish upon the national joy, and the favourite set-piece represents, as it should, a noble-hearted Yankee boy putting to flight a dozen stout red-jackets of King George.

Humour might suggest that the expression of Patriotism is a trifle overdone. Perhaps also a truce might be made with King George, who, if he be permitted to look from the shades upon a country which his Ministers lost, must surely smile at this immortality of resentment. But to the stranger, who witnesses this amazing carnival for the first time, two reflections occur. In the first place, the stranger cannot but be struck by the perfect adaptation of Jefferson's rodomontade to an expected purpose. Although that eminent Virginian, at the highest point of his exaltation, did not look forward to the inrush of foreigners which is overwhelming his country, there is a peculiar quality in his words, even when translated into Yiddish, which inspires an inexplicable enthusiasm. In the second place, the stranger is astounded at the ingenuity which inspires a crowd, separated by wide differences of race, speech, and education, with a sudden sympathy for a country which is not its own.

And when the last crackers are exploded, and the last flag is waved, what is left? An unreasoning conviction, cherished, as I have said, by a foreign population, that America is the greatest country on earth. What the conviction lacks in sincerity it gains in warmth of expression, and if America be ever confronted by an enemy, the celebrations of the Fourth of July will be found not to have been held in vain. Where there is no just bond of union, a bond must be invented, and Patriotism is the most notable invention of the great Republic. To have knit up all the nations of the earth in a common superstition is no mean achievement, and it is impossible to withhold a fervent admiration from the rhetoric which has thus attained what seemed, before its hour, the unattainable.

But in this cosmopolitan orgie of political excitement the true-born American plays but a small part. He has put the drama on the stage, and is content to watch the result. If a leader be needed in a time of stress, the man of Anglo-Saxon blood will be ready to serve the country, which belongs more intimately to him than to those who sing its praises with a noisy clatter. Meanwhile he lets the politicians do their worst, and watches the game with a careless indifference. Even if he loves his country, his love does not persuade him to self-sacrifice. You may measure his patriotism by the fact that, if he does venture upon a political career, his friends know not which they should do—praise him or condole with him. "Isn't it good of

So-and-so?" we constantly hear; "he has gone into politics." And with the approval is mixed a kindly, if contemptuous, sorrow. The truth is, that the young American of gentle birth and leisured ease hates to soil his hands with public affairs. His ambition does not drive him, as it drives his English cousin, into Parliament. He prefers to pursue culture in the capitals of Europe, or to urge an automobile at a furious pace across the sands. And the inaction of the real American is America's heaviest misfortune. So long as politics are left to the amateurs of graft, so long will Freedom be a fiction and Patriotism a piece of mere lip-service. Wealth is not wanting; brains are not wanting; energy is not wanting. Nothing is wanting save the inclination to snatch the control of the country from the hands of professional politicians. And until this control be snatched, it is idle to speak of reform. The Constitution of the United States is, we are told, a perfect Constitution. Its perfection is immaterial so long as Tammany on the one hand and the Trusts on the other conspire to keep it of no effect—a mere paper thing in a museum. The one thing needful is for men with clean hands and wise heads to govern their States, to stand for Congress, to enter the Senate, to defend the municipalities against corruption. And when this is done, the Declaration of Independence may safely be forgotten, in the calm assurance that it is better to spend one day in the service of patriotism than to fire off a thousand crackers and to dazzle the air with stars and stripes innumerable.

THE MILLIONAIRE.

The millionaire, or the multi-millionaire, if the plainer term be inadequate to express his lofty condition, is the hero of democratic America. He has won the allegiance and captured the imagination of the people. His antics are watched with envy, and described with a faithful realism of which statesmen are thought unworthy. He is hourly exposed to the camera; he marches through life attended by a bodyguard of faithful reporters. The trappings of his magnificent, if vulgar, existence are familiar to all the readers of the Sunday papers. His silver cars and marble palaces are the wonder of a continent. If he condescend to play golf, it is a national event. "The Richest Man on Earth drives from, the Tee" is a legend of enthralling interest, not because the hero knows how to drive, but because he is the richest man on earth. Some time since a thoughtless headline described a poor infant as "The Ten-Million-Dollar Baby," and thus made his wealth a dangerous incubus before he was out of the nursery. Everywhere the same tale is told. The dollar has a power of evoking curiosity which neither valour nor lofty station may boast. Plainly, then, the millionaire is not made of common day. Liquid gold flows in his veins. His eyes are made of precious jewels. It is doubtful whether he can do wrong. If by chance he does, it is almost certain that he cannot be punished. The mere sight and touch of him have a virtue far greater than that which kings of old claimed for themselves. He is at once the en-sample and the test of modern grandeur; and if, like a Roman emperor, he could be deified, his admiring compatriots would send him to the skies, and burn perpetual incense before his tomb.

Though all the millionaires of America are animated by the same desire,—the collection of dollars,—they regard their inestimable privileges with very different eyes. Mr Carnegie, for instance, adopts a sentimental view of money. He falls down in humble worship before the golden calf of his own making. He has pompously formulated a gospel of wealth. He piously believes that the millionaire is the greatest of God's creatures, the eloquent preacher of a new evangel. If we are to believe him, there is a sacred virtue in the ceaseless accumulation of riches. It is the first article in his creed, that the millionaire who stands still is going back, from which it follows that to fall behind in the idle conflict is a cardinal sin. A simple man might think that when a manufacturer had made sufficient for the wants of himself and his family for all time he might, without a criminal intent, relax his efforts. The simple man does not understand the cult. A millionaire, oppressed beneath a mountain of gold, would deem it a dishonour to himself and his colleagues if he lost a chance of adding to the weight and substance of the mountain.

Mr Carnegie, then, is inspired not by the romance but by the sentiment of gold. He cannot speak of the enormous benefits conferred upon the human race by the vast inequalities of wealth and poverty without a tear. "Millionaires," he says, "can only grow amid general prosperity." In other words, if there be not millions in the country the millionaire cannot put his hand upon them. That is obvious enough. His second text cannot be so easily accepted. "Their wealth is not made," he asserts dogmatically, "at the expense of their countrymen." At whose expense then is it made? Does Mr Carnegie vouch for the probity of all his colleagues? Does he cover with the aegis of his gospel the magnates of the Standard Oil Company, and that happy firm which, with no other advantage than a service of cars, levies toll upon the fruit-growers of America? Was the Steel Combine established without inflicting hardships upon less wealthy rivals? An answer to these simple questions should be given before Mr Carnegie's second text be inscribed upon the walls of our churches. It is not enough to say with Mr Carnegie that trusts obey "the law of aggregation." You need not be a Socialist to withhold your approval from these dollar-making machines, until you know that they were not established upon ruin and plunder. Even if the millionaire be the self-denying saint of modern times, it is still possible to pay too high a price for his sanctity and sacrifice.

It is the favourite boast of the sentimental millionaire that he holds his wealth in trust for humanity, — in other words, that he has been chosen by an all-wise Providence to be the universal almsgiver of mankind. The arrogance of this boast is unsurpassable. To be rich is within the compass of any man gifted or cursed with an acquisitive temperament. No one may give to another save in humbleness of spirit. And there is not a millionaire in America who does not think that he is fit to perform a delicate duty which has eluded the wise of all ages. In this matter Mr Carnegie is by far the worst offender. He pretends to take his "mission" very seriously. He does not tell us who confided the trust of philanthropy to him, but he is very sure that he has been singled out for special service. It is his modest pleasure to suggest a comparison with William Pitt. "He lived without ostentation and he died poor." These are the words which Mr Carnegie quotes with the greatest relish. How or where Mr Carnegie lives is his own affair; and even if he die poor, he should remember that he has devoted his life, not to the service of his country, but to the amassing of millions which he cannot spend. It is obvious, therefore, that the noble words which Canning dedicated to the memory of Pitt can have no meaning for him, and he would be wisely guided if he left the names of patriots out of the argument.

Mr Carnegie's choice of an epitaph is easily explained. He is wont to assert, without warrant, that "a man who dies rich dies disgraced." He does not tell us how the rich man shall escape disgrace. Not even the master of millions, great and good as he is reputed to be, knows when his hour comes. There is a foresight which even money cannot buy. Death visits the golden palace of the rich and the hovel of the poor with equal and unexpected foot. The fact that Mr Carnegie is still distributing libraries with both hands seems to suggest that, had he been overtaken during the last twenty years, he would not have realised his ideal. There is but one method by which a rich man may die poor, and that is by disencumbering himself of his wealth the very day that it is acquired. And he who is not prepared for this sacrifice does but waste his breath in celebrating the honour of a pauper's grave.

As there is no merit in living rich, so there is no virtue in dying poor. That a millionaire should desert his money-bags at his death is not a reproach to him if they be honestly filled. He has small chance of emptying them while he is on the earth. But Mr Carnegie has a reason for his aphorism. He aspires to be a philosopher as well as a millionaire, and he has decided that a posthumous bequest is of no value, moral or material. "Men who leave vast sums," says he, "may fairly be thought men who would not have left it at all had they been able to take it with them." On such a question as this the authority of Mr Carnegie is not absolute. Let the cobbler stick to his last. The millionaire, no doubt, is more familiar with account-books than with the lessons of history; and the record of a thousand pious benefactors proves the worth of wise legacies. Nor, indeed, need we travel beyond our own generation to find a splendid example of wealth honourably bestowed. The will of Cecil Rhodes remains a tribute to the generosity and to the imagination of a great man, and is enough of itself to brush aside the quibbles of Mr Carnegie.

The sentiment of "doing good" and of controlling great wealth leads rapidly to megalomania, and Mr Carnegie cannot conceal the pride of omniscience. He seems to think that his money-bags give him the right to express a definite opinion upon all things. He has distributed so many books, that perhaps he believes himself master of their contents. Though he has not devoted himself to politics or literature, he is always prepared to advise those who give themselves to these difficult arts. He has discovered that Greek and Latin are of no more practical use than Choctaw—which is perfectly true, if the useless money-bag be our *summum bonum*. With the indisputable authority of a man who keeps a large balance at his bank, he once dismissed the wars of the Greeks as "petty and insignificant skirmishes between savages." Poor Greeks! They did not pay their bills in dollars or buy their steel at Pittsburg. The chief article in his political creed is that monarchy is a crime. In his opinion, it is a degradation to kiss the King's hand. "The first man who feels as he ought to feel," says Mr Carnegie, "will either smile when the hand is extended at the suggestion that he could so demean himself, and give it a good hearty shake, or knock his Royal Highness down." In the same spirit of sturdy "independence" he urged the United States some years since to tax the products of Canada, because she "owes allegiance to a foreign power founded upon monarchical institutions." "I should use the rod," says the moneybag, "not in anger, but in love; but I should use it." Fortunately, it is not his to use; and his opinions are only memorable, since the country which he insults with his words is insulted also by his gifts. We may make too great a sacrifice in self-esteem, even for the boon of free libraries.

And with a hatred of monarchy Mr Carnegie combines a childlike faith in the political power of money. Though his faith by this should be rudely shaken, he clings to it as best he may. Time was when he wished to buy the Philippines, and present them, a free gift, to somebody or other. Now he thinks that he may purchase the peace of the world for a round sum, and sees not the absurdity of his offer. Even his poor attempt to bribe the English-speaking peoples to forget their spelling-books was a happy failure, and he still cherishes an illusion of omnipotence. At the opening of his Institute at Pittsburg he was bold enough to declare that his name would be known to future ages "like the name of Harvard." He might remember that Harvard gave not of his abundance. He bequeathed for the use of scholars a scholar's books and a scholar's slender savings, and he won a gracious immortality. Mr Carnegie, in endowing education, is endowing that which he has publicly condemned. Desiring to teach the youth of his country how to become as wealthy as himself, he has poured contempt upon learning. He has declared that "the college-made" man had "little chance against the boy who swept the office." He is to be found, this victim of an intellectual ambition, in the salaried class, from which the aspiring millionaire is bidden to escape as quickly as possible by the customary methods of bluff and bounce. Why, then, if Mr Carnegie thinks so ill of colleges and universities does he inflict his millions upon them? He has known "few young men intended for business who were not injured by a collegiate education." And yet he has done his best to drive all the youth of Scotland within the gates of the despised universities, and he has forced upon his own Pittsburg the gift of "free education in art and literature." Is it cynicism, or vain inconsequence? Cynicism, probably. The man who, having devoted his whole career to the accumulation of superfluous wealth, yet sings a paean in praise of poverty, is capable of everything. "Abolish luxury, if you please,"—thus he rhapsodises,—"but leave us the soil upon which alone the virtues and all that is precious in human character grow,—poverty, honest poverty!" Has he shed the virtues, I wonder; or is he a peculiarly sanctified vessel, which can hold the poison of wealth without injury?

Of all millionaires, Mr Carnegie is at once the least picturesque and the most dangerous. He is the least picturesque, because he harbours in his heart the middle-class ambition of philanthropy. He would undertake a task for which he is manifestly unfit, in the spirit of provincial culture. For the same reason he is the most dangerous. He is not content to squander his immense wealth in race-horses and champagne. He employs it to interfere with the lives of others. He confers benefits with a ready hand which are benefits only when they are acquired by conquest. Of a very different kind is Mr Thomas W. Lawson. He, too, is a millionaire. He, too, has about him all the appurtenances of wealth. His fur-coats are mythical. He once paid 30,000 dollars for a pink. "He owns a palace in Boston," says his panegyrist, "filled with works of art; he has a six-hundred acre farm in Cape Cod, with seven miles of fences; three hundred horses, each one of whom he can call by name; a hundred and fifty dogs; and a building for training his animals larger than Madison Square Garden." These eloquent lines will prove to you more clearly than pages of argument the native heroism of the man. He was scarce out of his cradle when he began to amass vast sums of money, and he is now, after many years of adventure, a king upon Wall Street. He represents the melodrama of wealth. He seems to live in an atmosphere of mysterious disguises, secret letters, and masked faces. His famous contest with Mr H. H. Rogers, "the wonderful Rogers, the master among pirates, whom you have to salute even when he has the point of his cutlass at the small of your back and you're walking the plank at his order," was conducted, on Mr Lawson's part, in the spirited style of the old Adelphi. "Mr Rogers' eyes snapped just once," we are told, on a famous occasion; but Mr Lawson was not intimidated. "I held myself together," he says proudly, "with closed hands and clinched teeth." Indeed, these two warriors have never met without much snapping of eyes and closing of hands and clinching of teeth. Why they snapped and closed and clinched is uncertain. To follow their operations is impossible for an outsider, but Mr Lawson always succeeds in convincing you that on the pretence of money-making he is attacking some lofty enterprise. He would persuade you that he is a knight-errant of purity. "Tremendous issues" are always at stake. The heroes of Wall Street are engaged in never-ending "battles." They are "fighting" for causes, the splendour of which is not dimmed in Mr Lawson's lurid prose. They have Americanised the language of ancient chivalry, until it fits the operations of the modern market. They talk of honour and of "taking each other's word," as though they had never stooped to dollars in their lives. But of one thing you may be sure — they are always "on hand when a new melon is cut and the juice runs out."

Like the knights of old, they toil not neither do they spin. They make nothing, they produce nothing, they invent nothing. They merely gamble with the savings of others, and find the business infinitely profitable. Yet they, too, must cultivate the language of sentiment. Though the world is spared the incubus of their philanthropy, they must pretend, in phrase at least, that they are doing good, and their satisfaction proves that nothing so swiftly and tranquilly lulls the conscience to sleep as the dollar. But, as the actor of melodrama falls far below the finished tragedian, the heroes of the Street, typified by Mr Lawson, are mere bunglers compared with the greatest millionaire on earth—John D. Rockefeller. We would no more give him the poor title of "Mr" than we would give it to Shakespeare. Even "Rockefeller" seems too formal for his grandeur. Plain "John D." is best suited to express the admiration of his worshippers, the general fame that shines like a halo about his head. He is Plutus in human guise; he is Wealth itself, essential and concrete. A sublime unselfishness has marked his career. He is a true artist, who pursues his art for its own sake. Money has given him nothing. He asks nothing of her. Yet he woos her with the same devotion which a lover shows to his mistress. Like other great men, Rockefeller has concentrated all his thoughts, all his energies, upon the single object of his desire. He has not chattered of things which he does not understand, like Mr Carnegie. He has resolutely refrained from Mr Lawson's melodramatic exaggeration. Money has been the god of his idolatry,—"*Dea Moneta*, Queen Money, to whom he daily offers sacrifice, which steers his heart, hands, affections—all."

His silence and his concentration give him a picturesqueness which his rivals lack. He stands apart from the human race in a chill and solitary grandeur. He seeks advertisement as little as he hankers after pleasure. The Sunday-school is his dissipation. A suburban villa is his palace. He seldom speaks to the world, and when he breaks his habit of reticence it is to utter an aphorism, perfect in concision and cynicism. "Avoid all honorary posts that cost time" — this was one of his earliest counsels to the young. "Pay a profit to nobody" is perhaps his favourite maxim. "Nothing is too small, for small things grow," is another principle which he formulated at the outset of his career. "I have ways of making money that you know nothing of," he once told a colleague, and no one will doubt the truth of his assertion. It is said that when he was scarce out of his teens he would murmur, with the hope of almost realised ambition, "I am bound to be rich, bound to be rich, bound to be rich." He imposed upon all those who served him the imperative duty of secrecy. He was unwilling that any one should know the policy of the Trust. "Congress and the State legislature are after us," he once said. "You may be subpoenaed. If you know nothing, you can tell nothing. If you know about the business, you might tell something which would ruin us." The mere presence of a stranger has always been distasteful to him. The custom of espionage has made him suspect that others are as watchful as himself. He has been described erroneously as a master of complicated villainy. He is, for evil or for good, the most single-minded man alive. He looks for a profit in all things. Even his devotion to the Sunday-school is of a piece with the test. "Put something in," says he, speaking of the work, "and according as you put something in, the greater will be your dividends of salvation."

His triumphant capture of the oil trade is a twice-told tale. All the world knows how he crushed his rivals by excluding their wares from the rail-roads, which gave him rebates, and then purchased for a song their depreciated properties. At every point he won the battle. He laid stealthy hands upon the pipe-lines, designed to thwart his monopoly, as he had previously laid hands upon the railway lines. He discovered no new processes, he invented no new methods of transport. But he made the enterprise of others his own. The small refiner went the way of the small producer, and the energy of those who carried oil over the mountains helped to fill Rockefeller's pocket. The man himself spared no one who stood between him and the realisation of his dream. Friends and enemies fell down before him. He ruined the widow and orphan with the same quiet cheerfulness wherewith he defeated the competitors who had a better chance to fight their own battle. The Government was, and is, powerless to stay his advance. It has instituted prosecutions. It has passed laws directed at the Standard Oil Company. And all is of no avail. Before cross-examining counsel, in the face of the court, Rockefeller maintains an impenetrable silence. He admits nothing. He confesses nothing. "We do not talk much," he murmurs sardonically; "we saw wood." A year ago it was rumoured that he would be arrested when he returned to America from Europe. He is still at large. The body of a multi-millionaire is sacred.

He is master of the world's oil, and of much else beside. Having won the control of one market, he makes his imperial hand felt in many another. His boast that "money talks" is abundantly justified. The power of money in making money is the only secret that the millionaires of America discover for themselves. The man who makes a vast fortune by the invention or manufacture of something which the people thinks it wants, may easily take a pride in the fruit of his originality. The captains of American industry can seldom boast this cause of satisfaction. It is theirs to exploit, not to create. The great day in Mr Carnegie's life was that on which "the mysterious golden visitor" came to him, as a dividend from another's toil. Mr Rockefeller remembers with the greatest pleasure the lesson which he learned as a boy, "that he could get as much interest for $50, loaned at seven per cent, as he could earn by digging potatoes ten days." The lesson of Shylock is not profound, but its mastery saves a world of trouble. Combined with a light load of scruples, it will fill the largest coffers; and it has been sufficient to carry the millionaires of America to the highest pinnacle of fame.

In other words, the sole test of their success is not their achievement, but their money-bags. And when, with cynical egoism, they have collected their unnumbered dollars, what do they do with them? What pleasures, what privileges, does their wealth procure? It is their fond delusion that it brings them power. What power? To make more money and to defy the laws. In England a wealthy man aspires to found a family, to play his part upon the stage of politics, to serve his country as best he may, and to prepare his sons for a like honourable service. The American millionaire does not share this ambition. Like Mr Rockefeller, he avoids "honorary posts." If he were foolish enough to accept them, he would not be loyal to the single desire of adding to his store. Perhaps we may best express his triumph in terms of champagne and oysters, of marble halls and hastily gathered collections. But even here the satisfaction is small. The capacity of the human throat is limited, and collections, made by another and partially understood, pall more rapidly than orchid-houses and racing-stables.

This, then, is the tragedy of the American multi-millionaires. They are doomed to carry about with them a huge load of gold which they cannot disperse. They are no wiser than the savages, who hide and hoard their little heaps of cowrie-shells. They might as well have filled their treasuries with flint-stones or scraps of iron. They muster their wealth merely to become its slave. They are rich not because they possess imagination, but because they lack it. Their bank-books are the index of their folly. They waste their years in a vain pursuit, which they cannot resist. They exclude from their lives all that makes life worth living, that they may acquire innumerable specimens of a precious metal. Gold is their end, not the gratification it may bring. Mr Rockefeller will go out of the world as limited in intelligence, as uninstructed in mind, as he was when he entered it. The lessons of history and literature are lost upon him. The joys for which wise men strive have never been his. He is the richest man on earth, and his position and influence are the heaviest indictment of wealth that can be made. His power begins and ends at the curbstone of Wall Street. His painfully gathered millions he must leave behind. Even the simple solace of a quiet conscience is denied to the most of his class. Is there one of them who is not haunted in hours of depression by the memory of bloody strikes, of honest men squeezed out, of rival works shut down?

In a kind of dread they turn to philanthropy. They fling from their chariots bundles of bank-notes to appease the wolves of justice. Universities grow ignobly rich upon their hush-money. They were accurately described three centuries ago by Robert Burton as "gouty benefactors, who, when by fraud and rapine they have extorted all their lives, oppressed whole provinces, societies, &c., give something to pious uses, build a satisfactory almshouse, school, or bridge, &c, at their last end, or before perhaps, which is no otherwise than to steal a goose and stick down a feather, rob a thousand to relieve ten." If America were wise she would not accept even the feather without the closest scrutiny. Money never loses the scent of its origin, and when the very rich explain how much they ought to give to their fellows, they should carry back their inquiry a stage farther. They should tell us why they took so much, why they suppressed the small factory, why they made bargains with railways to the detriment of others, why they used their wealth as an instrument of oppression. If their explanation be not sufficient, they should not be permitted to unload their gold upon a stricken country; they should not buy a cheap reputation for generosity with money that is not their own.

It may be said that the millionaire decrees the punishment for his own crimes. That is true enough, but the esteem in which America holds him inflicts a wrong upon the whole community. Where Rockefeller is a hero, a false standard of morals is set up. For many years he has preached a practical sermon upon the text, "The end justifies the means." How great are the means! How small the end! He has defended his harshest dealings on the ground that "it is business," and so doing has thrown a slur upon the commerce of his country. And, worse than this, the wonder and curiosity which cling about the dollar have created a new measure of life and character. A man is judged not by his attainments, his courage, his energy, but by his wealth. It is a simple test, and easily applied. It is also the poorest encouragement for the civic virtues. In England we help to correct the vulgarity of wealth by the distribution of titles, and a better aid than this could not be devised. Though the champions of democracy, who believe in equality of names as devoutly as in inequality of wealth, deem this old-fashioned artifice a shameful crime, it is not without its uses. It suggests that public service is worth a higher distinction than a mass of money. And, titles apart, it is happily not in accord with the traditions of our life to regard the rich man and the poor man as beings of a different clay and a different destiny. We may still echo without hypocrisy the words of Ben Jonson, "Money never made any man rich, but his mind."

THE AMERICAN LANGUAGE.

To the English traveller in America the language which he hears spoken about him is at once a puzzle and a surprise. It is his own, yet not his own. It seems to him a caricature of English, a phantom speech, ghostly but familiar, such as he might hear in a land of dreams. He recognises its broad lineaments; its lesser details evade, or confuse, him. He acknowledges that the two tongues have a common basis. Their grammatical framework is identical. The small change of language — the adverbs and prepositions, — though sometimes strangely used in America, are not strange to an English ear. And there the precise resemblance ends. Accent, idiom, vocabulary give a new turn to the ancient speech. The traveller feels as though he were confronted with an old friend, tricked out in an odd suit of clothes, and master of a new pose and unaccustomed gesture.

The Americans are commonly reputed to speak through their nose. A more intimate acquaintance with their manner belies this reputation. It is rather a drawl that afflicts the ear than a nasal twang. You notice in every sentence a curious shifting of emphasis. America, with the true instinct of democracy, is determined to give all parts of speech an equal chance. The modest pronoun is not to be outdone by the blustering substantive or the self-asserting verb. And so it is that the native American hangs upon the little words: he does not clip and slur "the smaller parts of speech," and what his tongue loses in colour it gains in distinctness.

If the American continent had been colonised by Englishmen before the invention of printing, we might have watched the growth of another Anglo-Saxon tongue, separate and characteristic. American might have wandered as far from English as French or Spanish has wandered from Latin. It might have invented fresh inflections, and shaped its own syntax. But the black art of Gutenberg had hindered the free development of speech before John Smith set foot in Virginia, and the easy interchange of books, newspapers, and other merchandise ensured a certain uniformity. And so it was that the Americans, having accepted a ready-made system of grammar, were forced to express their fancy in an energetic and a multi-coloured vocabulary. Nor do they attempt to belittle their debt, Rather they claim in English an exclusive privilege. Those whose pleasure it is to call America "God's own country" tell us with a bluff heartiness that they are the sole inheritors of the speech which Chaucer and Shakespeare adorned. It is their favourite boast that they have preserved the old language from extinction. They expend a vast deal of ingenuity in the fruitless attempt to prove that even their dialect has its roots deep down in the soil of classical English. And when their proofs are demanded they are indeed a sorry few. A vast edifice of mistaken pride has been established upon the insecure basis of three words—fall, gotten, and bully. These once were familiar English, and they are English no more. The word "fall," "the fall of the leaf," which so beautifully echoes the thought of spring, survives only in our provinces. It makes but a furtive and infrequent appearance in our literature. Chaucer and Shakespeare know it not. It is found in "The Nymph's Reply to the Shepherd":

> "A honey tongue, a heart of gall
> Is fancy's Spring, but Sorrow's Fall."

Johnson cites but one illustration of its use—from Dryden:

> "What crowds of patients the town-doctor kills,
> Or how last fall he raised the weekly hills."

On the other side of the Atlantic it is universally heard and written. There the word "autumn" is almost unknown; and though there is a dignity in the Latin word ennobled by our orators and poets, there is no one with a sense of style who will not applaud the choice of America.

But if she may take a lawful pride in "fall," America need not boast the use of "gotten." The termination, which suggests either wilful archaism or useless slang, adds nothing of sense or sound to the word. It is like a piece of dead wood in a tree, and is better lopped off. Nor does the use of "bully" prove a wholesome respect for the past. It is true that our Elizabethans used this adjective in the sense of great or noble. "Come," writes Ben Jonson in "The Poetaster," "I love bully Horace."[1] But in England the word was never of universal application, and was sternly reserved for poets, kings, and heroes. In modern America there is nothing that may not be "bully" if it meet with approval. "A bully place," "a bully boat," "a bully blaze,"—these show how far the word has departed from its origin. Nor, indeed, does it come down from English in an unbroken line. Overlooked for centuries, it was revived (or invented) in America some fifty years ago, and it is not to Dekker and Ben Jonson that we must look for palliation of its misuse.

Words have their fates. By a caprice of fortune one is taken, another is left. This is restricted to a narrow use; that wanders free over the plain of meaning. And thus we may explain many of the variations of English and of American speech. A simple word crosses the ocean and takes new tasks upon itself. The word "parlour," for instance, is dying in our midst, while "parlor" gains a fresh vigour from an increasing and illegitimate employment. Originally a room in a religious house, a parlour (or parloir) became a place of reception or entertainment. Two centuries ago an air of elegance hung about it. It suggested spinnets and powdered wigs. And then, as fashion turned to commonness, the parlour grew stuffy with disuse, until it is to-day the room reserved for a vain display, consecrated to wax-flowers and framed photographs, hermetically sealed save when the voice of gentility bids its furtive door be opened. The American "parlor" resembles the "parlour" of the eighteenth century as little as the "parlour" of the Victorian age. It is busy, public,

---

[1] Innumerable examples might be culled from the literature of the seventeenth century. One other will suffice here, taken from Dekker's "Shoemaker's Holiday ": "Yet I'll shave it off," says the shoemaker, of his beard, "and stuff a tennis-ball with it, to please my bully king."

and multifarious. It means so many things that at last it carries no other meaning than that of a false elegance. It is in a dentist's parlor that the American's teeth are gilded; he is shaved in a tonsorial parlor; he travels in a parlor-car; and Miss Maudie's parlor proves how far an ancient and respected word may wander from its origin. One example, of many, will illustrate the accidents which beset the life of words. No examples will prove the plain absurdity which has flattered the vanity of some American critics that their language has faithfully adhered to the tradition of English speech.

The vocabulary of America, like the country itself, is a strange medley. Some words it has assimilated into itself; others it holds, as it were, by a temporary loan. And in its choice, or invention, it follows two divergent, even opposite, paths. On the one hand, it pursues and gathers to itself barbarous Latinisms; on the other, it is eager in its quest after a coarse and living slang.

That a country which makes a constant boast of its practical intelligence should delight in long, flat, cumbrous collections of syllables, such as "locate," "operate," "antagonize," "transportation," "commutation," and "proposition," is an irony of civilisation. These words, if words they may be called, are hideous to the eye, offensive to the ear, and inexpressive to the mind. They are the base coins of language. They bear upon their face no decent superscription. They are put upon the street, fresh from some smasher's den, and not even the newspapers, contemptuous as they are of style, have reason to be proud of them! Nor is there any clear link between them and the meaning thrust upon them. Why should the poor holder of a season-ticket have the grim word "commutation" hung round his neck? Why should the simple business of going from one place to another be labelled "transportation"? And these words are apt and lucid compared with "proposition." Now "proposition" is America's maid-of-all-work. It means everything or nothing. It may be masculine, feminine, neuter—he, she, it. It is tough or firm, cold or warm, according to circumstances. But it has no more sense than an expletive, and its popularity is a clear proof of an idle imagination.

And while the American language is collecting those dried and shrivelled specimens of verbiage, it does not disdain the many-coloured flowers of lively speech. In other words, it gives as ready a welcome to the last experiment in Slang as to its false and pompous Latinisms. Nor is the welcome given in vain. Never before in the world's history has Slang flourished as it has flourished in America. And its triumph is not surprising. It is more than any artifice of speech the mark of a various and changing people. America has a natural love of metaphor and imagery; its pride delights in the mysteries of a technical vocabulary; it is happiest when it can fence itself about by the privilege of an exclusive and obscure tongue. And what is Slang but metaphor? There is no class, no cult, no trade, no sport which will not provide some strange words or images to the general stock of language, and America's variety has been a quick encouragement to the growth of Slang. She levies contributions upon every batch of immigrants. The old world has thus come to the aid of the new. Spanish, Chinese, German, and Yiddish have all paid their toll. The aboriginal speech of the Indians, and its debased lingo, Chinook, have given freely of their wealth. And not only many tongues but many employments have enhanced the picturesqueness of American Slang. America has not lost touch with her beginnings. The spirit of adventure is still strong within her. There is no country within whose borders so many lives are led. The pioneer still jostles the millionaire. The backwoods are not far distant from Wall Street. The farmers of Ohio, the cowboys of Texas, the miners of Nevada, owe allegiance to the same Government, and shape the same speech to their own purpose. Every State is a separate country, and cultivates a separate dialect. Then come baseball, poker, and the racecourse, each with its own metaphors to swell the hoard. And the result is a language of the street and camp, brilliant in colour, multiform in character, which has not a rival in the history of speech.

There remains the Cant of the grafters and guns, the coves that work upon the cross in the great cities. In England, as in France, this strange gibberish is the oldest and richest form of Slang. Whence it came is still a puzzle of the philologists. Harrison, in his 'Description of England' (1577), with a dogmatism which is not justified, sets a precise date upon its invention.

In counterfeiting the Egyptian rogues [says he of the vagabonds who then infested England], they have devised a language among themselves which they name Canting, but others Pedlars' French, a speech compact thirty years since of English, and a great number of odd words of their own devising, without all order or reason: and yet such is it that none but themselves are able to understand. The first deviser thereof was hanged by the neck,—a just reward, no doubt, for his deserts, and a common end to all of that profession.

The lingo, called indifferently Thieves' Latin or St Giles's Greek, was assuredly not the invention of one brain. The work of many, it supplied an imperious need. It was at once an expression of pride and a shield of defence. Those who understood it proved by its use that they belonged to a class apart; and, being unintelligible to the respectable majority, they could communicate with one another—secretly, as they hoped, and without fear of detection. Throughout the seventeenth and eighteenth centuries the flash tongue grew and was changed; it crossed the Atlantic with the early settlers, and it has left its marks upon the dialect of the American underworld. But its influence upon the common Slang has been light in America, as in England. It is as severely technical as the language of science, and is familiar chiefly to policemen, tramps, and informers. As Slang leaves the tavern and the street-corner, to invade the theatre, the office, and even the drawing-room, those who aim at a variety of speech need owe no debt to the Cant of the vagabonds, and it is not surprising that to-day the vulgar tongue, in America as in England, borrows more from "soldiers on the long march, seamen at the capstan, and ladies disposing of fish," than from the common cursetors and cony-catchers who once dominated it.

The use of Slang proves at once the wealth and poverty of a language. It proves its wealth when it reflects a living, moving image. It proves its poverty when it is nothing more than the vain echo of a familiar catchword.

At its best it is an ornament of speech; at its worst it is a labour-saving device. And it is for this reason that the vulgar American delights in the baser kind of

Slang: it seems to ensure him an easy effect He must be picturesque at all costs. Sometimes he reaches the goal of his ambition by a purposed extravagance. What can be more foolish than the description which follows of a man equal to the most difficult occasion: "He can light his cigar, when the battle is on, with the friction of a passing cannon-ball." In yet worse taste is another piece of fustian, invented by the same author: "When a 'twister' off the hills gets ready to do business in a 20-knot sou'wester it sends no messenger boys ahead to distribute its itinerary handbills." There is no fault of style which these few lines do not display. They combine, with a singular success, commonness and pomp. The epic poets of old were wont to illustrate the life of man by the phenomena of nature. The vulgar American reverses the process—he illustrates nature from the pavement.

Exaggeration, then, is one easy artifice of effect. Another is the constant repetition of certain words and phrases which have lost their meaning by detrition and are known to all. Not to be disappointed is sometimes as pleasant as to be surprised. A catchword passed from one to another is often a signal of sympathy, and many a man has been taken for a wit merely because his tinkling brain has given back the echo which was expected. In stereotyped phrases, in ready-made sentences, in the small change of meaningless words, the American language is peculiarly rich. "To cut ice," "to get next to," "straight goods,"[2]—these and similar expressions, of no obvious merit in themselves, long ago lost their freshness, and are not likely to assume a dignity with age. But they save trouble, they establish an understanding between him who speaks and him who hears; and when they are thrown into a discourse they serve the purpose of gestures, To exclaim "I should smile" or "I should cough" is not of much help in an argument, but such interjections as these imply an appreciation not merely of slang but of your interlocutor.

Slang is better heard than read. The child of the street or the hedgerow, it assumes in print a grave air which does not belong to it, or, worse still, it is charged with the vice or the vagabondage which it suggests. And so it is that Slang words have a life as closely packed with adventure as is the life of those who use them with the quickest understanding. To ask what becomes of last year's Slang is as rash as to speculate on the fate of last year's literature. Many specimens die in the gutter, where they were born, after living a precarious life in the mouths of men. Others are gathered into dictionaries, and survive to become the sport of philologists. For the worst of their kind special lexicons are designed, which, like prisons and workhouses, admit only the disreputable, as though Victor Hugo's definition—"L'argot, c'est le verbe devenu forçat"—were amply justified. The journals, too, which take their material where they find it, give to many specimens a life as long as their own. It is scarcely possible, for instance, to pick up an American

---

[2] To the Englishman who knows them not, the following quotations will explain their significance:—

"Tain't what ye ain't or what ye don't do that cuts ice with me."

"Well, invested capital has got to protect itself when the law won't do it. Ain't them straight goods?"

"Boston don't want Bishop Potter to come up here an' tell her 't she ain't next to the latest curves in goodness. Hully gee, no!"

newspaper that does not turn the word *cinch* to some strange purpose. The form and origin of the word are worthy a better fate. It passed from Spain into the Western States, and was the name given to saddle-girths of leather or woven horse-hair. It suggests Mexican horsemanship and the open prairie. The explanation given in the Century Dictionary will make clear its meaning to the untravelled: "The two ends of the tough cordage, which constitute the cinch, terminate in long narrow strips of leather called *latigos*, which connect the cinches with the saddle, and are run through an iron ring, called the *larigo* ring, and then tied by a series of complicated turns and knots, known only to the craft." In the West the word is still used in its natural and dignified sense. For example: "At Giles's ranch, on the divide, the party halted to cinch up." And then in the East it has become the victim of extravagant metaphor. As a verb, it means to hold firm, to put a screw on; as a noun, it means a grip or screw, an advantage fair or unfair. In the hand of the sporting reporter it can achieve wonders. "The bettor of whom the pool-room bookmaker stands in dread" — this flower of speech is culled from the 'New York World' — "is the race-horse owner, who has a cinch bottled up for a particular race, and drops into the room an hour or two before the race begins." The idea of bottling a cinch is enough to make a Californian shudder, and this confused image helps to explain the difference between East and West.

Thus words wander farther and farther from their origin; and when at last their meanings are wholly forgotten or obscured, they become part of the common speech. One kind of Slang may succeed to another, but cinch is secure for ever of a place in the newspaper, and in the spoken language, of America. Caboodle, also, is firmly established. The long series of words, such as Cachunk or Kerblunk, which suggest the impact of falling bodies with the earth, will live as expletives with Say, Sure, and many other, interjections which fill up the pauses of thought and speech. There are two other specimens of Slang beloved by the journals, for which it would be rash to prophesy a long life. To call a man or a thing or an act "the limit," is for the moment the highest step, save one, in praise or blame. When the limit is not eloquent enough to describe the hero who has climbed the topmost rung of glory, the language gasps into simplicity, and declares that he is It. "I didn't do a thing," says an eminent writer, "but push my face in there about eight o'clock last night, and I was It from the start." Though the pronoun is expressive enough, it does not carry with it the signs of immortality, and the next change of fashion may sweep it away into the limbo of forgotten words.

The journals do their best to keep alive the language of the people. The novelists do far more, since their works outlive by months or years the exaggeration of the press. And the novelists, though in narrative they preserve a scrupulous respect for the literary language, take what licence the dialect and character of their personages permit them. It is from novels, indeed, that future generations will best be able to construct the speech of to-day. With the greatest skill the writers of romance mimic the style and accent of their contemporaries. They put into the mouths of those who, in life, knew no other lingo, the highly-flavoured Slang of the street or the market. Here, for instance, is the talk of a saloon-keeper, taken from W. Payne's story, 'The Money Captain,' which echoes, as nearly as printed words can echo, the voice of the boodler:

"Stop it?" says the saloon-keeper of a journalist's attack. "What I got to stop it with? What's the matter with you fellows anyhow? You come chasin' yourselves down here, scared out of your wits because a dinky little one cent newspaper's makin' faces at you. A man 'd think you was a young lady's Bible-class and 'd seen a mouse.... Now, that's right," he exclaims, as another assailant appears; "make it unanimous. Let all hands come and rig the ship on old Simp. Tell him your troubles and ask him to help you out. He ain't got nothing better to do. Pitch into him; give him hell; he likes it. Come one, come all—all you moth-eaten, lousy stiffs from Stiffville. Come, tell Simp there's a reporter rubberin' around and you're scared to death. He'll sympathise with you—you sweet-scented skates."

It is not an elegant method of speech, but such as it is, it bears as close a resemblance to the dialect of Chicago as can be transferred from the ear to the eye.

If we compare the present with the past, we cannot but acknowledge that American Slang has grown marvellously in colour and variety. The jargon of Artemus Ward and Josh Billings possessed as little fire as character. These two humourists obtained their effect by the simple method, lately advocated by Messrs Roosevelt and Carnegie, of spelling as they pleased. The modern professors of Slang have invented a new style. Their pages sparkle with wit and allusion. They interpret their shrewd sense in words and phrases which have never before enjoyed the freedom of printer's ink. George Ade, the best of them all, has shown us how the wise ones of Chicago think and speak. His 'Fables in Slang' is a little masterpiece of humour in substance and wit in expression. To quote from it would be to destroy its effect. But it will discover the processes of Slang, as it is understood in the West, more clearly than any argument, and having amused the present generation, it will remain an historical document of enduring value.

Slang is the only language known to many thousands of citizens. The newly arrived immigrant delights to prove his familiarity with the land of his adoption by accepting its idioms and by speaking the American, not of books but of the market-place. And yet this same Slang, universally heard and understood, knocks in vain for admission into American literature. It expatiates in journals, in novels of dialect, and in works, like George Ade's, which are designed for its exposition. But it has no part in the fabric of the gravely written language. Men of letters have disdained its use with a scrupulousness worthy our own eighteenth century. The best of them have written an English as pure as a devout respect for tradition can make it. Though they have travelled far in space and thought, they have anchored their craft securely in the past. No writer that has handled prose or verse with a high seriousness has offended against the practice of the masters—save only Walt Whitman. The written word and the spoken word differ even more widely in America than elsewhere. The spoken word threw off the trammels of an uneasy restraint at the very outset. The written word still obeys the law of gradual development, which has always controlled it. If you contrast the English literature of to-day with the American, you will find differences of accent and expression so slight that you may neglect them. You will find resemblances which prove that it is not in vain that our literatures have a common origin and have followed a common road. The arts, in truth, are more willingly obedient than life or politics to the established order; and America, free and democratic though she be, loyally acknowledges the sovereignty of humane letters. American is heard at the street corner. It is still English that is written in the study.

AMERICAN LITERATURE.

There can, in fact, be no clearer proof that the tradition of literature is stronger than the tradition of life than the experience of America. The new world, to its honour be it said, has discovered no new art. The ancient masters of our English speech are the masters also of America. The golden chain of memory cannot be shaken off, and many of those who raise with the loudest voice the cry of freedom have shown themselves the loyal and willing slaves of the past.

The truth is that from the first the writers of America have lagged honourably behind their age. The wisest of them have written with a studious care and quiet reverence. As if to mark the difference between the written language and the vernacular, they have assumed a style which belonged to their grandfathers. This half-conscious love of reaction has been ever present with them. Tou may find examples at each stage of their history. Cotton Mather, who armed his hand and tongue against the intolerable sin of witchcraft, wrote when Dutch William was on our throne, and in style he was but a belated Elizabethan. There is no other writer with whom we may compare him, save Robert Burton, who also lived out of his due time. Take this specimen of his prose, and measure its distance from the prose of Swift and Addison, his younger contemporaries: "Wherefore the Devil," writes Mather in the simplicity of his faith, "is now making one Attempt more upon us; an Attempt more Difficult, more Surprising, more snarl'd with unintelligible Circumstances than any that we have hitherto Encountered; an Attempt so Critical, that if we get well through, we shall soon enjoy Halcyon Days with all the Vultures of Hell trodden under our feet." In sound and structure Mather's style is what the critics call "archaistic." It is all untouched by the influences of another world, and though "the New Englanders were," in Mather's view, "a People of God settled in those, which were once the Devil's Territories," they carried their prose from the old country, and piously bowed before an old tradition.

Thus has it been with each generation of men. Thoreau fondly believed that Walden had brought him near to nature, and he wrote with the accumulated artifice of the centuries. Hawthorne's language was as old in fashion as the Salem which he depicted, as "the grave, bearded, sable-cloaked, and steeple-crowned progenitor, who came so early with his Bible and his sword, and trode the common street with such stately port, and made so large a figure as a man of war and peace." But it was. upon Emerson that tradition has most strangely exercised its imperious sway. Now Emerson was an anarch who flouted the conventions of art and life. It was his hope to see the soul of this world "clean from all vestige of tradition." He did not understand that what is? proceeded inevitably from what was He affected to spurn the past as a clog upon his individuality. Anticipating Walt

Whitman, he would have driven away his nearest friends, saying, "Who are you? Unhand me: I will be dependent no more." So lightly did he pretend to esteem history that he was sure that an individual experience could explain all the ages, that each man went through in his own lifetime the Greek period, the medieval period—every period, in brief—until he attained to the efflorescence of Concord. "What have I to do with the sacredness of tradition," he asked proudly, "if I live wholly from within?" So much had he to do with it that he never wrote a line save in obedience. Savage as he was in the declaration of his own individuality, he expressed it in the gracious terms of an inherited art. To this age Emerson's provincialism appears sad enough. It would not have been remembered had it not been set forth in a finely studied and mellifluous prose. No sooner did Emerson take pen in hand than his anarchy was subdued. He instantly became the slave of all the periods which he despised. He was a faithful follower of the best models, a patient student of masters dead and gone. Though he aspired to live wholly from within, he composed his works wholly from without, and fashioned an admirable style for himself, more antique in shape and sound than the style affected by the Englishmen of his time. But it is Edgar Allan Poe who most eloquently preached the gospel of style, and who most honourably defended the cause of art pursued without the aid of the pulpit. Taste he declared to be the sole arbiter of Poetry. "With the intellect or the Conscience," said he, "it has only collateral relations. Unless incidentally it has no concern whatever either with Duty or Truth." Not that he belittled the exigence of Truth; he did but insist on a proper separation. "The demands of Truth," he admitted, "are severe; she has no sympathy with the myrtles. All that which is so indispensable in song is precisely all that with which she has nothing whatever to do." And thus it followed that he had small sympathy with Realism, which he denounced in the clear spirit of prophecy many years before it had become a battle-cry of criticism:

The defenders of this pitiable stuff [he wrote] uphold it on the ground of its truthfulness. Taking the thesis into question, this truthfulness is the one overwhelming defect. An original idea that—to laud the accuracy with which the stone is hurled that knocks us in the head. A little less accuracy might have left us more brains. And here are critics absolutely commending the truthfulness with which the disagreeable is conveyed! In my view, if an artist must paint decayed cheeses, his merit will lie in their looking as little like decayed cheeses as possible.

Of this wise doctrine Poe was always a loyal exponent. The strange veiled country in which he placed the shadows of his creation lay not within the borders of the United States. He was the child neither of his land nor of his century. Dwelling among men who have always worshipped size, he believed that there was no such thing as a long poem. A fellow-citizen of bustling men, he refused to bend the knee to industry. "Perseverance is one thing," said he, "genius quite another." And it is not surprising that he lived and died without great honour in his own country. Even those of his colleagues who guarded the dignity of their craft with a zeal equal to his own, shrank from the pitiless logic of his analysis. They loved his work as little as they respected his life. They judged him by a censorious standard which took no account of genius. And Poe shared with dignity and without regret the common fate of prophets. If he is still an exile in American esteem, he long since won the freedom of the larger world. He has been an inspiration to France, the inspirer of the nations. He did as much as any one of his contemporaries to mould the literary art of our day, and in the prose of Baudelaire and Mallarmé he lives a life whose lustre the indifference of his compatriots will never dim.

Whence comes it, this sedulous attention to style, which does honour to American literature? It comes in part, I think, from the fact that, before the triumph of journalism, American men of letters were secluded from their fellows. They played no *rôle* in the national drama. They did not work for fame in the field of politics. They were a band of aristocrats dwelling in a democracy, an *imperium in imperio*. They wrote their works for themselves and their friends. They made no appeal to the people, and knowing that they would be read by those capable of pronouncing sentence, they justified their temerity by a proper castigation, of their style. And there is another reason why American literature should be honourably formal and punctilious, If the written language diverges widely from the vernacular, it must perforce be studied more sedulously than where no such divergence is observed. For the American, accustomed to the language spoken by his countrymen and to the lingo of the daily press, literary English is an acquired tongue, which he studies with diligence and writes with care. He treats it with the same respect with which some Scots—Drummond, Urquhart, and Stevenson—have treated it, and under his hand it assumes a classic austerity, sometimes missed by the Englishman, who writes it with the fluency and freedom bred of familiar use. The stately and erudite work of Francis Parkman is a fair example. The historian of 'Montcalm and Wolfe' has a clear title to immortality. Assuredly he holds a worthy place among the masters. He is of the breed of Gibbon and Michelet, of Livy and Froude. He knows how to subordinate knowledge to romance. He disdains the art of narrative as little as he disdains the management of the English sentence. He is never careless, seldom redundant. The plainest of his effects are severely studied. Here, for instance, is his portrait of an Indian chief, epic in its simplicity, and withal composed with obvious artistry:

See him as he lies there in the sun, kicking his heels in the air and cracking jokes with his brother. Does he look like a hero? See him now in the hour of his glory, when at sunset the whole village empties itself to behold him, for to-morrow their favourite young partisan goes out against the enemy. His head-dress is adorned with a crest of war-eagle's feathers, rising in a waving ridge above his brow, and sweeping far behind him. His round white shield hangs at his breast, with feathers radiating from the centre like a star. His quiver is at his back; his tall lance in his hand, the iron point flashing against the declining sun, while the long scalp-locks of his enemies flutter from the shaft. Thus gorgeous as a champion in panoply, he rides round and round within the great circle of lodges, balancing with a graceful buoyancy to the free movements of his war-horse, while with a sedate brow he sings his song to the Great Spirit.

That is the language of classicism. The epithets are not far-sought. They come naturally to the mind. The hero's shield is round and white; his lance is tall; long are the scalp-locks of his enemies. Thus would Homer and Virgil have heightened the picture, and Park-man is clearly attentive to the best models. Even when he describes what his eye has seen he cannot disengage his impression from the associations of literature. It is thus that he sets before us Braddock's line of march:

It was like a thin, party-coloured snake, red, blue, and brown, trailing slowly through the depth of leaves, creeping round inaccessible heights, crawling over ridges, moving always in dampness and shadow, by rivulets and waterfalls, crags and chasms, gorges and shaggy steeps. In glimpses only, through jagged boughs and flickering leaves, did this wild primeval world reveal itself, with its dark green mountains, flecked with the morning mist, and its distant summits pencilled in dreamy blue.

As you read these words you are less keenly conscious of a visual impression than of a verbal effect, and it may be said without reserve that never for a page of his many volumes does Park-man forget the demands of dignity and restraint.

Excellent as is the style, it is never American. Parkman does not reveal his origin in a single phrase. He has learned to write not in his own land, but in the England of the eighteenth century. When he speaks of "the pampered Sardanapalus of Versailles," and of "the silken favourites' calculated adultery," we are conscious that he has learnt whatever lesson Gibbon has to teach. In other words, he, too, is obedient to the imperious voice of convention. And the novelists follow the same path as the historians. Mr Henry James, in his patient analysis of human character, has evoked such subtle harmonies as our English speech has not known before. Mr Howells, even when he finds his material in the land of his birth, shows himself the master of a classic style, exquisite in balance and perfect in tone. And both share the common inheritance of our tongue, are links in the central chain of our tradition, and in speech, if not in thought, are sternly conservative.

This, then, is an irony of America, that the country which has a natural dislike of the past still dances to the ancient measures, that the country which has invented so much has not invented a new method of expression, that the country which questions all things accepts its literature in simple faith. The advantages of conformity are obvious. Tradition is nine-tenths of all the arts, and the writers of America have escaped the ruin which overtakes the bold adventurer who stakes his all upon first principles. But sometimes we miss the one-tenth that might be added. How much is there in the vast continent which might be translated into words! And how little has achieved a separate, living utterance! Mr Stedman has edited an American Anthology, a stout volume of some eight hundred pages, whose most obvious quality is a certain technical accomplishment. The unnumbered bards of America compose their verses with a diffident neatness, which recalls the Latin style of classical scholars. The workmanship is deft, the inspiration is literary. If many of the authors' names were transposed small injustice would be done them. The most of the work might have been written anywhere and under any conditions. Neither sentiment nor local colour suggests the prairie or the camp.

It is the intervention of dialect which alone confers a distinctive character upon American verse. Wisely is Mr Stedman's collection called an Anthology. It has something of the same ingenuity, the same impersonality, which marks the famous Anthology of the Greeks; it illustrates the temper not of a young but of an old people.

How shall we surprise in her literature the true spirit of America? Surely not in Walt Whitman, whose work is characteristic not of his country, but of himself, who fondly believed that he would make a loud appeal to the democracy because he stamped upon the laws of verse, and used words which are not to be found in the dictionary. Had the people ever encountered his 'Leaves of Grass,' it would not have understood it. The verse for which the people craves is the ditties of the music-hall. It has no desire to consider its own imperfections with a self-conscious eye. It delights in the splendour of mirrors, in the sparkle of champagne, in the trappings of a sordid and remote romance. The praise of liberty and equality suits the ear not of the democrat, but of the politician and dilettante, and it was to the dilettante and politician that Walt Whitman addressed his exhortations. Even his studied contempt for the literary conventions is insincere, and falls away from Kim when he sees and feels most vividly. He attempted to put into practice Emerson's theory of anarchy. He was at the pains to prove that he was at once a savage and a poet. That he had moments of poetic exaltation is true. The pomp of Brooklyn Ferry lives in his stately verse.

But he was no savage. It was his culture that spoke to the culture of others; it was a worn-out commonplace which won him the regard of politicians. He inspired parodists, not poets. And he represented America as little as he echoed the voice of the people.

Nor is it in the works of the humourists that we shall catch a glimpse of the national character. They, too, cast no shadow but their own. They attain their effects by bad spelling, and a simple transliteration reveals the poverty of their wit. There is but one author who represents with any clarity the spirit of his country, and that author is Mark Twain. Not Mark Twain the humourist, the favourite of the reporters, the facile contemner of things which are noble and of good report, but Mark Twain, the pilot of the Mississippi, the creator of Huck Finn and Tom Sawyer. He is national as Fielding is national. Future ages will look upon Huck Finn as we look upon Tom Jones,—as an embodiment of national virtue. And Mark Twain's method is his own as intimately as the puppets of his imagining. It is impossible to read a page of his masterpieces without recognising that they could have been composed only in an American environment. The dialect in which they are written enhances their verisimilitude without impairing their dignity; and the flashes of humour which light up the gravity of the narrative are never out of place nor out of tune. The cunning and resourcefulness of his boyish heroes are the cunning and resourcefulness of America, and the sombre Mississippi is the proper background for this national epic. The danger, the excitement, the solemnity of the great river are vividly portrayed. They quicken his narrative; they inspire him to eloquence. He remembers with a simple enthusiasm the glory of the sun setting upon its broad expanse; he remembers also that the river and its shoals are things to fear and to fight.

Fully to realise the marvellous precision [he writes] required in laying the great steamer in her marks in that murky waste of water, one should know that not only must she pick her intricate way through snags and blind reefs, and then shave the head of the island so closely as to brush the overhanging foliage with her stern, but at one place she must pass almost within arm's reach of a sunken and visible wreck that would snatch the hull timbers from under her if she should strike it, and destroy a quarter of a million dollars' worth of steamboat and cargo in five minutes, and maybe a hundred and fifty human lives into the bargain.

In calm, as in flood, Mark Twain has mastered the river, and has made it his own. Once upon a time the Mississippi called up a vision of the great Gulf opening on the sight of La Salle, "tossing its restless billows, limitless, voiceless, lonely as when born of chaos, without a sail, without a sign of life." Now a humbler image is evoked, and we picture Huck Finn and Jim floating down the broad stream in the august society of the Duke and the Dauphin.

Though Mark Twain cultivates the South-Western dialect, and does not disdain the speech of Pike County, there is in his two romances no suspicion of provincialism. Style and imagination give them the freedom of the whole world. They are of universal truth and application. But since the days of Huck Finn and Tom Sawyer the conditions of American literature have changed, and for the worse. As in England, so in America, a wide diffusion of books, an eager and general interest in printed matter, have had a disastrous effect. The newspapers, by giving an improper advertisement to the makers of books, have rendered the literary craft more difficult of pursuit. The ambition of money has obscured the simple end of literature, and has encouraged a spirit of professionalism eminently characteristic of a practical country. We hear of works of fiction sketched in the back-offices of publishers, whose hands are held upon the public pulse. All is arranged, we are told, by the man of business—period, plot, characters. Nothing is left to the novelist but to carry out the instructions of his taskmaster, and when you contemplate the result you can feel no surprise at this composite authorship. It is no better than a money-making partnership, a return to the miserable practices of Grub Street and its hacks, a curiosity of trade, not of art, and so long as its sorry product is distinguished from genuine literature no great harm is done.

Of the modern tendencies which affect literature, not commerce, the most conspicuous is the tendency to decentralise. Every province has its coterie, every county its school The whole continent is pegged out in well-acknowledged claims. Boston cultivates one style, Chicago another. Each corner makes the most of its own material, and cheerfully discovers to the other States its character and temperament. The result is of great and varied interest. The social history of America is being written piecemeal, and written often with a skill and sincerity which merit the highest praise. And not merely has each province found its chronicler, but the immigrants, also, are intent upon self-expression. The little masterpieces of Abraham Cahan are an earnest of what the Ghetto can achieve, and whether the Jews are faithful to Yiddish, or, like Cahan, acquire the language of their adopted country, there is no reason why they should not atone in a free land for centuries of silence. To enumerate the manifold achievements of the States is impossible. One example will suffice, and no city will better suit my purpose than Chicago. That admirable literature should come from Chicago is of itself a paradox. It is still more surprising that the best writers of Chicago should display the qualities of tranquillity and reticence, which you would expect least of all to find in that monstrous city. Yet it is characteristic of Miss Edith Wyatt and Mr H. B. Fuller, who have painted the manners of Chicago with the greatest skill, that they never force the note. They look upon their fellow-citizens with an amiable sympathy; they describe them with a quiet humour. It is true that they have an excellent opportunity. It is true also that they rise to their occasion. Within the limits of Chicago are met the most diverse of men. On the one hand are the captains of industry, intent to amass a fortune at all costs; on the other are the sorry prigs who haunt Ibsen clubs and chatter of Browning. Miss Wyatt, with an exquisite irony, makes clear her preference. In her eyes the square-dealing and innocent boodler is a far better man than the sophisticated apostle of culture, and this truth she illustrates with a modesty and restraint which are rarely met with in modern fiction. She never insists; she never says a word too much. With exquisite concision she sets her carefully selected facts and types before you, and being the antithesis of priggishness in a priggish city, she glorifies "the common growth of Mother Earth," and compels your agreement. Her collection of stories—'Every One His Own Way'—as free from pretence as from exaggeration, paints the citizens of Chicago with the subtlest fancy and the simplest truthfulness.

Mr H. B. Fuller employs an ampler canvas. His intention is the same. He also discards the artifice of exaggeration. He attempts to harrow your feelings as little as to advertise himself. He displays not the *sæva indignatio*, which won another novelist of Chicago so indiscreet a fame. He is for gentler methods and plainer judgments. In 'The Cliff Dwellers' he has given us a picture of the tribe inhabiting the Clifton, a monstrous sky-scraper full eighteen stories tall, whose "hundreds of windows," he tells you, "glitter with multitudinous letterings in gold and in silver, and on summer afternoons its awnings flutter score on score in the tepid breezes that sometimes come up from Indiana." His picture is never overcharged; his draughtsmanship is always sincere. He knows the tribe with an easy familiarity, and he bears witness to their good and their evil with perfect impartiality. He is never a partisan. His portraits are just, and he leaves his reader to sum up the qualities of each. At his hands Chicago suffers no injury. She does not return his generosity. A prophet is not without honour save in his own country, and when I asked for his books at the biggest bookshop in Chicago, I was met with a stare of ignorance.

And what you find in Chicago you may find in New England, in Kentucky, in California, everywhere. The curiosity of this vast continent tempts its writers to explore. Their material varies with the locality of their choice. Their skill is a common inheritance. They cultivate the graces as carefully as did their predecessors. Their artistic conscience is no less acute. Above all, they have brought the short story to a point of singular perfection. If Edgar Poe showed them the way, they have proved themselves apter disciples than any save the most skilful of Frenchmen.

It is, indeed, impossible to look forward to the future of American literature without hopefulness. In that half-discovered country style and invention go hand in hand. The land of Mr Howells and Frank Norris, of Mrs Atherton and Mrs

Wharton, of Stephen Crane and Harold Frederic, has accomplished so much that we may look confidently for the master, who in his single achievement will knit up its many diverse qualities and speak to the world with the voice of America.

THE UNDERWORLD.

Nowhere and at no time, save in the England of the eighteenth century, was the underworld so populous or so popular as in the America of to-day. In life, as in letters, crime and criminals hold there a lofty place. They are the romance of the street and the tenement-house. In their adventure and ferocity there is a democratic touch, which endears them to a free people. Nor are they so far remote from the world of prosperity and respect in the cities of the United States as elsewhere. The police is a firm and constant link between criminal and politician. Wherever the safe-blowers and burglars are, there you will find stool-pigeons and squealers,[3] ready to sell their comrades for liberty and dollars. And if the policeman is the intimate of the grafter, he is the client also of the boss who graciously bestowed his uniform upon him. At chowder parties and picnics thief, policeman, and boss meet on the terms of equality imposed upon its members by the greatest of all philanthropic institutions—Tammany Hall. If you would get a glimpse into this strange state within a state, you have but to read the evidence given before the Lexow Committee[4] in 1894. It would be difficult to match the cynicism and brutality there disclosed.

In every line of this amazing testimony you may detect a contempt of human life and justice, an indifference to suffering, an eager lust after unearned dollars, which are without parallel. The persons who play their part in this austere, begrimed tragi-comedy, come for the most part from oversea, and have but a halting knowledge of the language spoken by judges and senators. Yet their very ignorance stamps their speech with authenticity, and enhances its effect. The quick dialogue is packed with life and slang. Never were seen men and women so strange as flit across this stage. Crook and guy, steerer and turner, keepers of gambling-hells and shy saloons, dealers in green-goods,[5] come forward with their eager stories of what seems to them oppression and wrong.

With the simplicity which knows no better they deplore their ill-rewarded "industry," and describe their fraudulent practices as though they were a proper means of earning bread and butter. They have as little shame as repentance. Their only regrets are that they have been ruined by the police or forced to spend a few barren years in the State prison. And about them hover always detective and police-captain, ill-omened birds of prey, who feed upon the underworld. There is

---

[3] A stool-pigeon is a thief in the pay of the police; a squealer is a grafter who betrays his brother.

[4] This strange collection of documents, a whole literature in itself, bears the prosaic title, "Investigations of the Police Department of the City of New York."

[5] Forged dollar-notes.

nothing more remarkable in this drama of theft and hunger than the perfect understanding which unites the criminal lamb and the wolfish upholder of the law. The grafter looks to his opponent for protection, and looks not in vain, so long as he has money in his pocket. The detective shepherds the law-breakers, whom he is appointed to arrest; he lives with them; he shares their confidences and their gains; he encourages their enterprise that he may earn a comfortable dividend; and he gives them up to justice when they are no longer worth defending. No dramatist that ever lived could do justice to this astounding situation, and it is the highest tribute to human ingenuity that few of the interlocutors fall below their opportunity.

And it may be admitted that New York gave, and gives, an easy chance to policemen bent upon oppression. What can the poor, ignorant foreigners, who throng the east side of the city, do against their brutal and omnipotent guardians? "An impressive spectacle was presented to us one day," reports the Committee, "in the presence of about 100 patrolmen in uniform, who during the period of three preceding years had been convicted by the police commissioners of unprovoked and unwarranted assault on citizens." Still more impressive than "this exhibit of convicted clubbers" was "a stream of victims of police brutality who testified before the Committee. The eye of one man, punched out by a patrolman's club, hung on his cheek. Others were brought before the Committee, fresh from their punishment, covered with blood and bruises, and in some cases battered out of recognition." The whole city seemed the prey of a panic terror. One day "a man rushed into the session, fresh from an assault made upon him by a notorious politician and two policemen, and with fear depicted upon his countenance threw himself upon the mercy of the Committee and asked its protection, insisting that he knew of no court and of no place where he could in safety go and obtain protection from his persecutors." From all which it is plain that too high a price may be paid for the philanthropy of Tammany Hall, and that a self-governing democracy cannot always keep an efficient watch upon its guardians.

What is it in the life and atmosphere of America which thus encourages crime, or rather elevates crime to a level of excellence unknown elsewhere? In the first place, the citizens of New York are the disciples of Hobbes. To them life is a state of war. The ceaseless competition for money is a direct incentive to the combat. Nature seems to have armed every man's hand against his fellow. And then the American is always happiest when he believes himself supreme in his own walk. The man who inhabits the greatest country on earth likes to think of his talent as commensurate with his country's. If he be a thief, he must be the most skilful of his kind; if he be a blackmailing policeman, he must be a perfect adept at the game. In brief, restlessness and the desire of superiority have produced a strange result, and there is little doubt that the vulgar American is insensitive to moral shocks. This insensitiveness is easily communicated to the curious visitor. A traveller of keen observation and quick intelligence, who has recently spent "a year amongst Americans," accepts the cynicism of the native without a murmur. After yielding to that spirit of enthusiastic hope which is breathed by the Statue of Liberty, he thus discusses the newly-arrived alien:

Even the stars in their courses [thus he writes] fight for America, if not always for the immigrant when he lands. The politicians would fain prevent his assimilation in order that his vote might be easily manipulated by them; but first of all he must have a vote to be handled, and to this end the politicians provide him with naturalisation papers, fraudulent it may be—the State Superintendent of Elections in New York estimates that 100,000 fraudulent naturalisation papers were issued in New York State alone in 1903,—and thus in the very beginning of his life in America the immigrant feels himself identified with, and takes delight and pride in, the American name and nature; and lo! already the alien is bound to the "native" by the tie of a common sentiment, the ἦθος of the Greeks, which is one of the most powerful factors of nationality.

Poor ἦθος! many follies have been spoken in your name! But never before were you identified with fraudulent naturalisation! Never before were you mistaken for the trick of a manipulating politician!

Such being the tie of a common sentiment, it is not surprising that the Americans are universally accustomed to graft and boodle. With characteristic frankness they have always professed a keen interest in those who live by their wits. It is not for nothing that Allan Pinkerton, the eminent detective, called affectionately "the old man," is a national hero. His perfections are already celebrated in a prose epic, and he is better known to west as to east than the President himself. And this interest, this sense of heroism, are expressed in a vast and entertaining literature. Nowhere has this literature of scoundrelism, adorned by Defoe and beloved by Borrow, flourished as it has flourished in America. Between the dime novel and the stern documents of the Lexow Committee there is room for history and fiction of every kind. The crooked ones of the earth have vied with the detectives in the proper relation of their experiences. On the one hand you find the great Pinker-ton publishing to the world a breathless selection from his own archives; on the other, so practised a novelist as Mr Julian Hawthorne embellishing the narrative of Inspector Byrnes; and it is evident that both of them satisfy a general curiosity. In these records of varying merit and common interest the attentive reader may note the changes which have taken place in the method and practice of thieving. There is no man so ready to adapt himself to new circumstances as the scoundrel, and the ingenuity of the American rogue has never been questioned. In the old days of the backwoods and romance Jesse James rode forth on a high-mettled steed to hold up cars, coaches, and banks; and James Murel, the horse-thief, celebrated by Mark Twain, whose favourite disguise was that of an itinerant preacher, cherished no less a project than an insurrection of negroes and the capture of New Orleans. The robber of to-day is a stern realist. He knows nothing of romance. A ride under the stars and a swift succession of revolver-shots have no fascination for him. He likes to work in secret upon safe or burglar-box. He has moved with the times, and has at his hand all the resources of modern science. If we do not know all that is to be known of him and his ambitions it is our own fault, since the most expert of his class, Langdon W. Moore, has given us in 'His Own Story of his Eventful Life' (Boston, 1893) a complete revelation of a crook's career. It is an irony of life that such a book as this should come out of Boston, and yet it is so quick in movement, of so breathless an excitement, that it may outlive many specimens of Bostonian lore and culture. It is but one example out of many, chosen because in style as in substance it outstrips all competitors.

Without knowing it, Langdon W. Moore is a disciple of Defoe. He has achieved by accident that which the author of 'Moll Flanders' achieved by art. There is a direct simplicity in his narrative which entitles him to a place among the masters. He describes hair-breadth escapes and deadly perils with the confident air of one who is always exposed to them. He gives the impression of the hunted and the hunter more vividly than any writer of modern times. When he is opening a safe, you hear, in spite of yourself, the stealthy step upon the stair. If he watches for a pal at the street end, you share his anxiety lest that pal should be intercepted by the watchful detective. And he produces his effects without parade or ornament. He tells his story with a studied plainness, and by adding detail to detail keeps your interest ever awake. Like many other great men, he takes his skill and enterprise for granted. He does not write of his exploits as though he were always amazed at his own proficiency. Of course he has a certain pride in his skill. He cannot describe his perfect mastery over all the locks that ever were made without a modest thrill. He does not disguise his satisfaction at Inspector Byrnes' opinion that "he had so deeply studied combination locks as to be able to open them from the sound ejected from the spindle." For the rest, he recognises that he is merely a workman, like another, earning his living, and that nothing can be accomplished save by ceaseless industry and untiring toil. Like many another hero, Langdon W. Moore was born in New England, and was brought up at Newburyport, a quiet seaport town. The only sign of greatness to be detected in his early life was an assault upon a schoolmaster, and he made ample atonement for this by years of hard work upon a farm. He was for a while a typical hayseed, an expert reaper, ready to match himself against all comers. He reached his zenith when he was offered fifty dollars in gold for six weeks' toil, and he records with a justified pleasure that "no man had ever been paid such high wages as that." But his energetic spirit soon wearied of retirement, and he found his way to New York, not to be fleeced, like the hayseed of the daily press, but to fleece others. The gambling hells knew him; he became an adept at poker and faro; and he soon learned how to correct or to compel fortune. His first experiment was made upon one Charley White, who dealt faro bank every Saturday night; and it is thus that Moore describes the effect of an ingenious discovery:

He kept his box and cards in a closet adjoining his room. One night during his absence I fitted a key to his closet, took out his cards, and sand-papered the face of eight cards in each deck. I then removed the top of his faro-box, bulged out the centre of the front plate at the mouth, and filed the plate on the inside at both corners to a bevel. I then replaced the top, put in a deck of cards, and made a deal. I found the cards not sanded would follow up and fill the mouth of the box after each turn was made; and if the mouth remained dark and the edge of the top card could not be seen, one of the sand-papered cards was next, and a loser. This would give me several "dead" turns in each deal.

By this means the great man, still despised as a Boston bean-eater, was able to bring his adversary to ruin. The adversary at last discovered the artifice, and "for the next five years," to quote Moore's own words, "we met as strangers."

It will be seen that from his earliest days Moore possessed a scientific ingenuity, which the hard experience of life rapidly improved. And it was not long before a definite direction was given to his talent. Arrested in 1856, as he thought unjustly, he determined "to do no more work until obliged to do it for the State." He therefore turned his skill of hand to account, and went into the "green goods business." His success in this venture was so great that he made the best dollar bills ever put upon the market, and he boasts legitimately that in the game he "never lost a man." Presently he discovered that there was a quicker profit in stolen bonds. "From my first venture in this bond-smashing business," to quote his own simple words, "in 1862 up to 1870, I made more money than in any branch of industry I was ever engaged in." "Branch of industry" is admirable, and proves that Moore had a proper appreciation of his craft. But bond-smashing compelled a perfect knowledge of locks and bolts, and in this knowledge, as has been said, Moore was supreme. At the end of his career, when he had hung his arms upon the wall, and retired to spend a green old age at Boston, it was to his treatment of Yale and Lillie locks that he looked back with the greatest pleasure. But no exploit flattered his vanity more easily than the carrying off from the Bank at Concord—the Concord of Emerson and Hawthorne—of some three hundred thousand dollars. That he purchased his freedom by an ample restitution mattered nothing to the artist. His purpose was achieved, his victory won, and if his victims came by their own again, he at least had the satisfaction which comes of a successful engagement.

Of this adventure he writes with more enthusiasm than he is wont to show. He wishes his readers to understand that it was not a sudden descent, but the culmination of five months' steady work. He had watched the bank until he knew the habits of its manager and the quality of its locks. He "was satisfied from all he saw that by hard persistent work the bank could be cleaned out completely." It was on a July day in 1867 that the scheme first took shape in Moore's mind. He had stopped at noon at the hotel at Concord for food, and saw the cashier of the bank returning from his dinner.

The bank had been closed during his absence [thus he tells his simple story], and he now unlocked the street door and left the key in the lock. I followed him upstairs and saw him unlock the outer and inner doors of the vault, and also the door of the burglar-box. I presented a hundred-dollar note and asked to have it changed. Being accommodated, I left the place, observing as I went out that the lock on the street door was a heavy one of the familiar tumbler variety, and that it had a wooden back.

Thus the train was laid, and in three months came the explosion. Impressions were taken of locks, keys were provided, a waggon and team were held in readiness, and one day as the cashier left the bank to get his dinner, Langdon W. Moore, with a meal-bag concealed under his vest, quietly opened the front door and entered the bank. One check he knew. As he went in a girl of twelve tried to follow him—a near relative of the cashier. The exercise of a little tact satisfied her that the directors were in session, and she ran off to her playmates under the big elm at the opposite corner of the street. Moore lost no time in locking the door behind him, in opening all the locks, which yielded to his cunning and foresight, and in packing the meal-bag full of bonds, bank-notes, and plate. He accomplished the deed without haste, and by the time that the cashier had finished his dinner Moore had disappeared with his bag, and his waggon, and his friends, and left no trace behind.

Another masterpiece, in Moore's opinion, was what he magniloquently calls the great robbery of an express car. Here, too, he proved the fineness of his craft. He left nothing to chance, and he foresaw, with the coolness of a practised hand, every step which his adversaries would take. His first care was to obtain the assistance of the messenger who travelled on the car which he proposed to rob, and the zeal and energy wherewith he coached his accomplices ensured success. Again and again he rehearsed every scene in the comedy. Before his eyes the messenger was attacked by two masked ruffians, of whom one caught him by the throat, while the other put a pistol to his head, saying, "If you open your mouth I will blow a hole through your head large enough for a pigeon to fly through." Then the messenger was gagged and bound, a piece of soap was put into his mouth, that he might appear in the last extremity, and presently he was set to learn by heart the tale that he should tell his employers. By long practice each actor became perfect in his part. The car was raided, one hundred and sixty-five thousand dollars was the modest spoil, and Pinkerton and his men were gallantly defied. A hasty trip to Canada still further perplexed the pursuers, and if we may believe Moore, he not only baffled the great detective, but persuaded the Express Company to dispute his claim. Moore, in fact, took a sportsman's as well as an artist's pleasure in the game. After the discomfiture of his enemies, he loved nothing better than a neat job. He professes a frank delight in explaining how once upon a time he opened the Honourable Benjamin Wood's safe, and did not soil his carpet. And there was good reason for his scruple. No sooner had he flashed his dark lantern on the office than he observed that the floor was newly covered, and that fresh paint and paper shone upon the walls. Now he had no objection to easing the Honourable Benjamin of fifty thousand dollars. Being a gentleman, he would scorn to spoil a new Brussels carpet. Accordingly he took some papers from Mr Wood's file and spread them carefully on the floor. The rest of the dramatic recital shall be given in his own words:

When this was done, we drilled two five-eighth-inch holes through the fireproof door into the bolt·case, jacked the plate from the frame,... and opened the door. I then put in a wooden wedge at the top to keep the plate from springing back, took down the jack, and shook out all the loose filing upon the papers. This I gathered carefully up, and put the lime, plaster, and papers in the coal-hod, placed some more clean papers under the door, and made everything ready to leave the building as soon as the boodle was transferred safe to our pockets. After looking through the books and papers, the money was taken out and counted. It amounted to but a single one-dollar note.

Was ever an artist so bitterly deceived? Langdon W. Moore rose to the occasion. He was no pilferer, and scorned to carry off so mean a booty. In the words of the police-captain, he would not add larceny to burglary. But he paid the penalty of greatness. His work was instantly recognised. "I know the man," said Captain Jordan, "for there is but one in the world who would take all that trouble to save your carpet while breaking open your safe."

It reminds you of the story told by Pliny of Apelles the painter, who once upon a time called upon Protogenes, another master of his craft, when Protogenes was not within. Whereupon Apelles, seeing a picture before him, took a pencil and drew in colour upon the picture a passing fine and small line. Then said he to the old woman in the house, "Tell thy master that he who made this line inquired for him." And when Protogenes returned, and had looked upon the line, he knew who had been there, and said withal, "Surely Apelles has come to town, for it is impossible that any but he should make in colour so fine workmanship." Thus genius is betrayed by its own perfection, and he who refused to soil the carpet could not but be recognised by his skill.

And Langdon W. Moore was forced to pay another and a more grievous penalty for his renown. As the fame of his prowess spread abroad, he fell a prey to the greed of detectives. Do what he would, he could never rid himself of the attentions of the police. Henceforth it was almost impossible for him to work in safety, and whatever booty he obtained he must needs share with his unwelcome companions. He was like a fly condemned to spend his life in the irk-some society of the spider. When he had not much to give, his poverty was rewarded by years in prison; and then, as he says himself, he "was welcomed back into the old criminal life by crooked police officials." These officials had no desire to help him. "I was not asked by them"—again it is Moore who speaks—"if I was in want of anything, but was told that if I wanted to make some money they could put me on to a good bank job where I could make a million." And, if we may believe the historians, Moore's experience is not singular. The truth is, the thief-taker still flourishes in America. Jonathan Wild, his occupation gone in England, has crossed the ocean, and plies his trade with greater skill and treachery than ever. He thinks it better to live on the criminal than to catch him. And thus he becomes a terror not to the evildoer but to the law-abiding citizen. It is his business to encourage crime, not to stamp it out. If there were no thieves, where would the stool-pigeon and detective find their profits? "W'y," said a pickpocket[6] in New York, "them coppers up there in the Tenderloin couldn't have any diamond rings if we didn't help to pay for 'em. No, they couldn't. They'd sit down in the street and actually cry—an' they're big men some of 'em—if we guns was run off the earth." In other words, the lesson of the American Underworld is that the policeman may be a far greater danger to the community than the criminal. Jonathan Wild will always do more harm than Jack Sheppard. The skill and daring of the cracksman makes him a marked man. But *quis custodes custodiet?*

---

[6] See 'The World of Graft,' by J. Flint (1901), p. 154.

EPILOGUE.

A traveller visiting a strange land takes for granted the simpler virtues. He notes with gratitude and without surprise the generous practice of hospitality. He recognises that the husbandman, patiently toiling on his farm, *adscriptus glebæ*, holds in his toil-worn hands the destiny of his country. He knows that the excellent work done in tranquil seclusion by men of letters and scholars will outlast the braggart achievements of well-advertised millionaires and "prominent" citizens. Fortunately, such virtues as these are the common inheritance of all peoples.

They are not characteristic of this nation or of that. They belong, like air and sunlight, to the whole civilised world. And it is not by similarities, but by differences, that the traveller arrives at a clear picture of a foreign land. Especially in America do the softer shades and quieter subtleties escape the unaccustomed eye. The swift energies, the untiring restlessness, the universal haste, obscure the amenities of life more darkly there than elsewhere. The frank contempt of law and blood, which receives a daily illustration, must needs take a firmer hold of the observer than the peaceful tillage of the fields and the silent acquisition of knowledge. America is unhappy in that she is still making her history, not one episode of which a vigilant and lupine press will suffer to go unrecorded. Graft and corruption stalk abroad, public and unashamed. The concentration of vast wealth in a few pockets results, on the one hand, in a lowering of the commercial code, on the other, in a general diffusion of poverty, These are some of the traits which mark America off from the other nations, and these traits none with a sense of the picturesque can ever overlook.

Yet it is not these traits which make the deepest impression upon the returning traveller. As he leaves the shores of America he forgets for the moment her love of money and of boodle, he forgets her superb energy and hunger for life, he forgets the exquisite taste shown by the most delicately refined of her citizens. He remembers most vividly that he is saying good-bye to the oldest land on earth. It is an irony of experience that the inhabitants of the United States are wont to describe themselves as a young people. They delight to excuse their extravagances on the ground of youth. When they grow older (they tell you) they will take another view of politics and of conduct. And the truth is that old age long ago overtook them. America is not, never was, young. She sprang, ready-made, from the head of a Pilgrim Father, the oldest of God's creatures. Being an old man's daughter, she has escaped the virtues and vices of an irresponsible childhood. In the primitive history of the land her ancestors took no part. They did not play with flint-knives and set up dolmens where New York now stands. They did not adorn themselves with woad and feathers. The Prince Albert coat (or its equivalent) was always more appropriate to their ambition. In vain you will search the United States for the signs of youth. Wherever you cast your eye you will find the signal proofs of an eager, grasping age. Youth loiters and is glad, listening to the songs of birds, wondering at the flowers which carpet the meadow, and recking not of the morrow. America is grave and in a hurry. She is not content to fleet the time carelessly, as they did in the golden age. The one hope of her citizens is to get to Wall Street as quickly as possible, that they may add to their already useless hoard of dollars. For this purpose they have perfected all those material appliances which increase the rapidity and ease of life. They would save their labour as strenuously as they would add to their fortunes. A telephone at every bed-head has made the toil of letter-writing superfluous. A thousand ingenious methods of "transportation" have taken away the necessity of walking. There is no reason why in the years to come hand and foot should not both be atrophied. But there is nothing young in this sedulous suppression of toil. Youth is prodigal of time and of itself. Youth boasts of strength and prowess to do great deeds, not of skill to pile millions upon millions, a Pelion upon an Ossa of wealth. Nor in the vain luxury of New York can we detect anything save the signs of age. It is only in modern America that the mad extravagance of Nero's Rome may be matched. There the banquet of Trimalchio might be presented without surprise and without reproach. It differs from what are known as "freak dinners" only in the superiority of its invention and in the perfection of its table-talk.

In brief, the fantastic ambition of a "cottage" at Newport, as of Trimalchio's villa in Southern Italy, is the ambition, not of primitive, reckless, pleasure-loving youth, but of an old age, sated and curious, which hurries to decay.

Again, it is not a young people which cries aloud "too old at forty!" In the childhood of the world, the voice of age is the voice of wisdom. It is for Nestor that Homer claims the profoundest respect, and to-day America is teaching us, who are only too willing to learn the baneful lesson, that knowledge and energy die with youth. Once upon a time I met an American who had returned from his first visit to Europe, and when I asked what was the vividest impression he brought from thence, he replied: "I was surprised to see an old man like the German Emperor doing so much work." In our more youthful eyes the German Emperor has but crossed the threshold of life. The years of his mature activity lie before him, we believe, like an untrodden road. But for the American, prematurely worn out by the weight of time and the stress of affairs, William II. already hastens to his decline, and clings to the reins of office with the febrile courage of an old man.

And all the while America is sublimely unconscious that the joys of childhood are not hers. Though with the hypochondria of advancing years she demands a doctor for her soul, she knows not from what disease she suffers. She does not pray for a Medea to thrust her into a cauldron of rejuvenescence. With a bluff optimism she declares that she is still the youngest of the nations, and boasts that when she has grown up to the height of her courage and activity she will make triumphant even her bold experiment in democracy. Not upon her has the divine injunction descended: Γνῶθι σεαυτὸν. She who knows so much knows not herself. How should she, when she is composed of so many and so diverse elements? And lacking self-knowledge, she lacks humour. With the best will in the world, she cannot see the things about her in a true proportion. The blithe atmosphere, clear as crystal, sparkling as champagne, in which she lives, persuades her to take a too serious and favourable view of her own character. And let it be remembered that with her optimism she still treasures the sentimentality of her Puritan ancestors. She is a true idealist, who loves nothing so dearly as "great thoughts." She delights in the phrases and aspirations which touch the heart more nearly than the head. Though her practice does not always square with her theory, especially in the field of politics, she is indefatigable in the praise of freedom, equality, and the other commonplaces of democracy. The worst is, that she cannot laugh at herself. Her gravity and sensitiveness still lie, like stumbling-blocks, in her path. She accepts the grim adulation of such unwise citizens as Mr Carnegie as no more than her due. If only she could dismiss the flattery of her admirers with an outburst of Gargantuan hilarity, all virtues might be added unto her. But, as I have said, she lacks this one thing. She is the home of humourists and no humour. A thousand jesters minister to her amusement, and she pays them handsomely. More jokes are made within her borders in a day than suffice the rest of the globe for a year. And the laughter which they provoke is not spontaneous. You can hear the creak of the machine as it goes to work. The ever-present jester is a proof that humour is an exotic, which does not grow naturally on the soil, and does not belong more intimately to the American people than did the cumbersome jokes of Archie Armstrong to the monarch who employed him. The humour which simplifies life, and detects a spice of ridicule even in the operations of business and politics, is rarely found in America. Nor is its absence remarkable. The Americans are absorbed from early youth to ripe old age in the pursuit of success. In whatever path they walk they are determined to triumph. Sport for them is less an amusement than a chance to win. When they embark upon business, as the most of them do, their ambition is insatiable. They are consumed by the passion of money-making. The hope of victory makes them despise toil and renounce pleasure. Gladly will they deprive themselves of rest and lead laborious lives. The battle and its booty are their own reward. They count their gathered dollars with the same pride wherewith the conquering general counts his prisoners of war. But the contest marks their faces with the lines of care, and leaves them beggared of gaiety. How can they take themselves other than seriously when millions depend upon their nod? They have bent their energies to one special end and purpose—the making of money; and in the process, as an American once said to me, they forget to eat, they forget to live. More obviously still, they forget to laugh. The comedy of their own career is never revealed to them. Their very slang displays their purpose: they are "out for the stuff," and they will not let it escape them. A kind of sanctity hangs about money. It is not a thing to be taken lightly; it is no proper subject for a jest. And as money and its quest absorb the best energies of America, it follows that America is distinguished by a high seriousness with which Europe is powerless to compete. However far a profession may be removed from the mart, profit is its end. Brilliant research, fortunate achievement—these also are means, like buying and selling. In scholarship, as in commerce, money is still the measure of success. Dr Münsterberg, a well-known professor at Harvard, has recorded the opinion of a well-known English scholar, which, with the doctor's comment, throws a clearer light upon the practice of America than a page of argument. "America will not have first-class scholarship," said the Englishman, "in the sense in which Germany or England has it, till every professor in the leading universities has at least ten thousand dollars salary, and the best scholars receive twenty-five thousand dollars." Dr Münsterberg refused at first to accept this conclusion of the pessimist, but, says he, the years have convinced him. Scholars must be paid generously in the current coin, or they will not respect their work. It is not greed, precisely, which drives the American along the road of money-getting. It is, as I have said, a frank pride in the spoils, a pride which is the consistent enemy of light-heartedness, and which speedily drives those whom it possesses into a grave melancholy.

This, then, is the dominant impression which America gives the traveller—the impression of a serious old gentleman, whom not even success will persuade to laugh at his own foibles. And there is another quality of the land, of which the memory will never fade. America is apprehensive. She has tentacles strong and far-reaching, like the tentacles of a cuttle-fish. She seizes the imagination as no other country seizes it. If you stayed long within her borders, you would be absorbed into her citizenship and her energies like the enthusiastic immigrant.

You would speak her language with a proper emphasis and a becoming accent. A few weeks passed upon her soil seem to give you the familiarity of long use and custom. "Have I been here for years?" you ask after a brief sojourn. "Can it be possible that I have ever lived anywhere else?"

Lector House believes that a society develops through a two-fold approach of continuous learning and adaptation, which is derived from the study of classic literary works spread across the historic timeline of literature records. Therefore, we aim at reviving, repairing and redeveloping all those inaccessible or damaged but historically as well as culturally important literature across subjects so that the future generations may have an opportunity to study and learn from past works to embark upon a journey of creating a better future.

This book is a result of an effort made by Lector House towards making a contribution to the preservation and repair of original ancient works which might hold historical significance to the approach of continuous learning across subjects.

HAPPY READING & LEARNING!

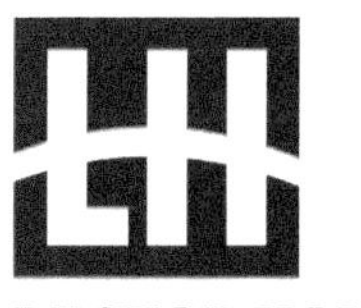

LECTOR HOUSE LLP
E-MAIL: lectorpublishing@gmail.com